BORDEAUX TRAVEL GUIDE 2023 AND BEYOND

An Unforgettable Travel Companion for Exploring the Jewel of France and Beyond in 2023 and Beyond

MAXIMILIAN HARTLEY

2

3

Copyright © 2023 by Maximilian Hartley

All rights reserved.
No part of this book may be reproduced,
distributed, or transmitted in any form
or by any means, including
photocopying, recording, or other
electronic or mechanical methods,
without the prior written permission of
the publisher, except in the case of brief
quotations embodied in critical reviews
and certain other noncommercial uses
permitted by copyright law.

Unauthorised duplication, distribution,
or transmission of this book is a
violation of applicable laws and may
result in severe civil and criminal
penalties. Legal action will be taken
against individuals or entities found to
be in breach of copyright.

Introduction to Bordeaux

1.1 Overview of Bordeaux

1.2 History of Bordeaux

1.3 Geographical Location and Climate

1.4 Getting to Bordeaux

1.5 Getting Around Bordeaux

Planning Your Trip to Bordeaux

2.1 Best Time to Visit Bordeaux

2.2 Duration of Stay

2.3 Budgeting for Your Trip

2.4 Accommodation Options

Exploring Bordeaux City

3.1 Bordeaux City Center

3.1.1 Place de la Bourse

3.1.2 Cathédrale Saint-André

3.1.3 Porte Cailhau

3.1.4 La Cité du Vin

3.2 Historic Neighborhoods

3.2.1 Saint Pierre District

3.2.2 Saint-Michel District

3.2.3 Chartrons District

3.3 Museums and Galleries

3.3.1 Musée d1'Aquitaine

3.3.2 CAPC Musée d'Art Contemporain

3.3.3 Musée du Vin et du Négoce

3.4 Parks and Gardens

Wine Tourism in Bordeaux

4.1 Bordeaux Wine Regions

4.2 Wine Tasting and Tours

4.3 Wine Museums and Education Centers

Day Trips from Bordeaux

5.1 Arcachon

5.2 Dune du Pilat

5.3 Saint-Émilion

5.4 Cognac

5.5 Médoc Wine Route

Gastronomy in Bordeaux

6.1 Bordeaux Culinary Delights

6.2 Best Restaurants in Bordeaux

6.3 Markets and Food Experiences

Outdoor Activities in Bordeaux

7.1 Cycling and Bike Paths

7.2 Water Sports on the Garonne River

7.3 Golfing in Bordeaux

7.4 Hiking and Nature Trails

7.5 Adventure Parks and Recreation

Shopping in Bordeaux

8.1 Shopping Districts

8.2 Local Products and Souvenirs

Events and Festivals in Bordeaux

9.1 Bordeaux Wine Festival

9.2 Bordeaux Fête le Fleuve

9.3 Bordeaux International Fireworks Competition

9.4 Bordeaux Marathon

9.5 Other Cultural and Music Festivals

Practical Information

10.1 Emergency Contacts

10.2 Useful Phrases

10.3 Safety Tips

10.4 Transportation Information

10.5 Local Customs and Etiquette

Conclusion

Introduction to Bordeaux

Overview of Bordeaux

Bordeaux is a renowned wine region located in southwestern France. It is considered one of the most prestigious and influential wine regions in the world, known for producing some of the finest and most sought-after wines. Bordeaux's winemaking history dates back centuries, with its vineyards and wineries steeped in tradition and craftsmanship.

Geographically, Bordeaux is situated on the banks of the Garonne River, which eventually merges with the Dordogne River to form the Gironde estuary. This unique location creates a favorable climate for grape cultivation, as the rivers moderate temperatures and create a maritime influence that is conducive to viticulture.

Bordeaux is divided into several sub-regions, each with its own distinct terroir and winemaking traditions. The Left Bank, or the "Rive Gauche," is situated on the west side of the Gironde estuary and is known for producing predominantly Cabernet Sauvignon-based wines. The prestigious communes of Médoc and Graves are located here, and they are home to some of Bordeaux's most esteemed châteaux, including Château Margaux, Château Latour, and Château Haut-Brion.

On the Right Bank, or the "Rive Droite," the dominant grape variety is Merlot. This region includes famous appellations such as Saint-Émilion and Pomerol, where Merlot-based wines with rich, velvety textures and complex flavors are produced. Château Cheval Blanc and Château Pétrus are among the notable estates found on the Right Bank.

Apart from the Left and Right Banks, Bordeaux also encompasses several other important sub-regions. The region of Graves, located south of the city of Bordeaux, produces both red and white wines, with the latter being particularly renowned. The sweet white wines of Sauternes and Barsac, made from grapes affected by the noble rot, are also highly prized and considered some of the world's finest dessert wines.

The Bordeaux region boasts a wide range of grape varieties. While Cabernet Sauvignon, Merlot, and Sauvignon Blanc are the most commonly grown, other permitted red grape varieties include Cabernet Franc, Malbec, and Petit Verdot, while Sémillon and Muscadelle are often blended with Sauvignon Blanc for white wines. Bordeaux winemakers are known for their expertise in blending different grape varieties to achieve complexity, balance, and longevity in their wines.

The Bordeaux winemaking process is meticulous and carefully controlled to maintain the quality and reputation of the region. The wines are classified into various categories, including the prestigious Bordeaux Wine Official Classification of 1855, which ranked the top Châteaux of the Médoc and Sauternes. The classification remains largely unchanged to this day and is a testament to the historical significance and excellence of Bordeaux's wines.

Bordeaux wines are celebrated for their exceptional aging potential, with many of the top estates producing wines that can evolve and improve over several decades. The region's wines often exhibit characteristics such as deep color, concentrated fruit flavors, complex aromas, and a harmonious balance of tannins and acidity.

In recent years, Bordeaux has embraced modern winemaking techniques while also honoring its traditional methods. Many estates have implemented sustainable practices, organic farming, and precision viticulture to preserve the environment and produce wines of exceptional quality.

Bordeaux's global reputation has led to the establishment of a vibrant wine tourism industry. Visitors can explore the picturesque vineyards, tour the prestigious châteaux, and taste a wide range of wines. Bordeaux also hosts the Vinexpo, one of the world's largest wine trade fairs, attracting wine professionals and enthusiasts from around the globe.

In conclusion, Bordeaux is an iconic wine region that epitomizes excellence, tradition, and innovation in winemaking. Its diverse terroir, meticulous craftsmanship, and historic classification systems have contributed to its status as a benchmark for quality wines. Whether it is a red from the Left Bank, a Merlot-based gem from the Right Bank, or a luscious Sauternes, Bordeaux offers a captivating and unforgettable wine experience.

History of Bordeaux

Bordeaux is a renowned wine region located in southwestern France, known for producing some of the world's finest wines. The history of Bordeaux stretches back centuries, with the region playing a significant role in the development of the wine industry and shaping the global wine market. From its early beginnings to the present day, Bordeaux has consistently been a symbol of prestige and excellence in winemaking.

Early History:
The origins of winemaking in Bordeaux can be traced back to the ancient Roman period. The Romans established a settlement called

Burdigala in the 3rd century BC, which served as a thriving port city along the Garonne River. The favorable climate and fertile soil of the region proved ideal for viticulture, and vine cultivation quickly became widespread.

Middle Ages and English Influence:
During the Middle Ages, Bordeaux's wine trade expanded significantly. In the 12th century, the region came under English rule through the marriage of Eleanor of Aquitaine to King Henry II of England. The English developed a strong taste for Bordeaux wines and began exporting them to England, initiating a long-standing relationship between Bordeaux and the British market.

The 18th and 19th Centuries:
The 18th century brought a period of prosperity and innovation to Bordeaux's wine industry. The region experienced advancements in winemaking techniques, such as the introduction of glass bottles and the use of cork stoppers, which helped preserve the quality of the wines during transportation. Bordeaux wines gained popularity across Europe and became a favorite among nobles and aristocrats.

In the 19th century, Bordeaux faced challenges such as the phylloxera epidemic, which devastated vineyards across Europe. The crisis led to the replanting of vineyards using disease-resistant American rootstocks. Despite the setbacks, the Bordeaux wine industry rebounded, and vineyard owners implemented modern techniques to improve the quality and consistency of their wines.

Classification Systems:
Bordeaux's reputation as a top wine-producing region was solidified in the 1855 Bordeaux Wine Official Classification. Emperor Napoleon III requested a classification of Bordeaux wines for the Exposition Universelle de Paris, and as a result, the wines of Bordeaux were ranked based on their perceived quality. The classification included five growths, or "crus," ranging from Premier Cru (first growth) to Cinquième Cru (fifth growth), with the famous Château Lafite Rothschild and Château Margaux among the Premier Crus.

In addition to the 1855 Classification, several other classification systems have been established in Bordeaux, such as the Classification of Saint-Émilion and the Crus Bourgeois classification in the Médoc region.

These classifications help consumers navigate the diverse range of wines produced in Bordeaux and provide a benchmark for quality.

Modern Era and Global Recognition:
In recent decades, Bordeaux has continued to evolve and adapt to changing consumer preferences and market demands. Winemakers have embraced sustainable viticulture practices and modern winemaking techniques while preserving the traditional character of Bordeaux wines. The region's diverse terroir, encompassing gravelly soils near the Garonne River and clay-limestone soils in the eastern areas, contributes to the unique flavors and characteristics found in Bordeaux wines.

Today, Bordeaux is recognized as one of the most prestigious wine regions in the world. It produces a wide array of wines, ranging from dry reds and whites to sweet dessert wines. The region's appellations, such as Médoc, Saint-Émilion, Pauillac, and Pessac-Léognan, are synonymous with exceptional quality and craftsmanship.

Conclusion:
The history of Bordeaux is intertwined with the development of the global wine industry. From

its early Roman roots to the influential English period and the establishment of classification systems, Bordeaux has consistently played a central role in shaping the world of wine. With its rich heritage, commitment to quality, and diverse range of wines, Bordeaux continues to captivate wine enthusiasts and connoisseurs worldwide.

Geographical Location and Climate

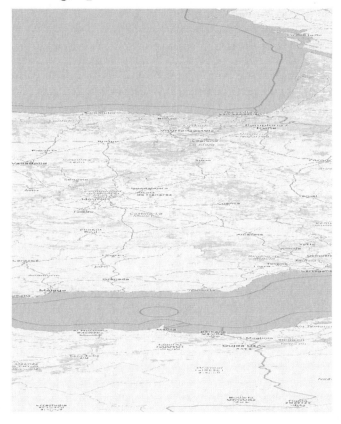

Bordeaux, often referred to as the "wine capital of the world," is a renowned wine region located in southwestern France. With its rich viticultural history, picturesque landscapes, and diverse terroir, Bordeaux has earned a reputation for producing some of the finest wines in the world. Understanding the geographical location and climate of Bordeaux is crucial for comprehending the unique characteristics and quality of the wines it produces.

Geographical Location:
Bordeaux is situated in the Aquitaine region of France, along the banks of the Garonne River. It occupies a vast area of approximately 120,000 hectares (297,000 acres), making it one of the largest wine-growing regions globally. The region is divided into several sub-regions, including Médoc, Saint-Émilion, Pomerol, Graves, and Sauternes, each with its distinctive terroir and wine styles.

The region's proximity to the Atlantic Ocean greatly influences its climate and viticulture. Bordeaux enjoys a maritime climate, characterized by mild winters, moderate rainfall, and warm summers. The oceanic influence brings cooling breezes and helps moderate temperature extremes, creating favorable conditions for grape cultivation.

Climate:
Bordeaux experiences a temperate climate, heavily influenced by the nearby Atlantic Ocean and the presence of the Gironde

Estuary. The region benefits from the Gulf Stream, which provides a warming effect and regulates the overall temperature.

The climate in Bordeaux is classified as oceanic or maritime, with mild winters and relatively warm summers. However, there are variations in climate across the sub-regions due to their different geographical features. In general, Bordeaux has a long growing season, allowing grapes to ripen gradually and develop complex flavors.

The annual rainfall in Bordeaux is moderate, averaging around 900 millimeters (35 inches) per year. This rainfall is evenly distributed throughout the year, ensuring a consistent water supply for the vines. The proximity to the ocean also results in higher humidity levels, which can pose challenges such as the development of vine diseases like mildew and botrytis.

Bordeaux experiences significant diurnal temperature variations, with cooler nights and warmer days during the growing season. This diurnal shift helps maintain acidity levels in the grapes while allowing them to reach optimal ripeness during the day.

The terroir of Bordeaux is incredibly diverse, owing to variations in soil types, elevations, and microclimates within the region. The Left Bank, which includes the Médoc and Graves sub-regions, is known for its gravelly soils that provide excellent drainage and heat reflection. The Right Bank, encompassing Saint-Émilion and Pomerol, features more clay and limestone soils, promoting water retention and offering a different expression of the grapes.

In conclusion, Bordeaux's geographical location and climate play a significant role in shaping the region's viticulture and the distinctive character of its wines. The maritime climate, with its moderating influence from the Atlantic Ocean, creates favorable conditions for grape cultivation, allowing for a long growing season and gradual ripening of the grapes. The diverse terroir across the sub-regions of Bordeaux further adds to the complexity and variety of the wines produced in this renowned wine region.

Getting to Bordeaux

Bordeaux, located in southwestern France, is a vibrant city renowned for its rich history, exquisite architecture, and world-class vineyards. Whether you are a wine enthusiast, a history buff, or simply seeking a charming destination, Bordeaux offers a perfect blend of cultural heritage, culinary delights, and picturesque landscapes. In this guide, we will provide you with detailed information on how to get to Bordeaux, ensuring a smooth and convenient journey to this captivating city.

By Air:
Bordeaux is well-connected to major cities worldwide through its international airport, Bordeaux-Mérignac Airport (BOD). The airport serves numerous airlines, offering both

domestic and international flights. It has direct connections to cities like Paris, London, Amsterdam, Barcelona, and Frankfurt, among others. From the airport, you can easily reach the city center using various transport options such as taxis, airport shuttles, or public buses.

By Train:
France has an extensive and efficient rail network, and Bordeaux is no exception. The city is served by the Gare de Bordeaux Saint-Jean, the main train station located in the city center. High-speed trains, such as the TGV (Train à Grande Vitesse), connect Bordeaux with major French cities like Paris (approximately 2 hours), Lyon, Marseille, and Toulouse. Additionally, there are international train connections to cities in neighboring countries, including Spain, Belgium, Switzerland, and Italy. The train station is well-connected to the city center through tram lines, buses, and taxis.

By Car:
If you prefer the flexibility of driving, Bordeaux is easily accessible by car. The city is well-connected to the French motorway network, making it convenient to reach from various directions. The A10 motorway links Bordeaux

with Paris, while the A63 connects it with Spain and the A89 with Lyon. Driving to Bordeaux allows you to explore the scenic countryside and vineyards at your own pace. However, keep in mind that parking in the city center can be limited and expensive, so it's advisable to use public transportation or park in designated areas outside the center.

By Bus:
Bordeaux has excellent bus connections with other French cities and some international destinations. Several long-distance bus companies operate routes to and from Bordeaux, providing affordable options for travelers. The main bus station in Bordeaux is the Gare Routière de Bordeaux-Saint-Jean, which is located adjacent to the train station. From there, you can easily access the city center using public transportation.

By Boat:
For a unique and leisurely approach to Bordeaux, you can consider traveling by boat along the Garonne River. Several river cruise companies offer scenic cruises that take you from other European cities to Bordeaux. These cruises provide an opportunity to admire the picturesque landscapes and vineyards along

the river, immersing you in the beauty of the region.

Once you arrive in Bordeaux, you will find a well-connected public transportation system consisting of trams, buses, and taxis, allowing you to explore the city and its surroundings with ease. Bordeaux's compact city center is best explored on foot, as many of its attractions, including the historic district, shopping areas, and renowned monuments, are within walking distance of each other.

In conclusion, Bordeaux is easily accessible through various means of transportation. Whether you choose to arrive by air, train, car, bus, or even by boat, getting to Bordeaux is a convenient and enjoyable experience. The city's excellent transportation infrastructure ensures that you can start your Bordeaux adventure with ease, immersing yourself in the rich culture, heritage, and renowned wines that this remarkable city has to offer.

Getting Around Bordeaux

Bordeaux, located in the southwest of France, is a beautiful city renowned for its historical architecture, world-class wine, and vibrant cultural scene. As the capital of the Nouvelle-Aquitaine region, Bordeaux offers a wide array of attractions and experiences for visitors. To make the most of your time in Bordeaux, it's important to familiarize yourself with the various transportation options available in the city. In this guide, we will explore the different ways to get around Bordeaux efficiently and conveniently.

Tramway:
The tramway system in Bordeaux is one of the most efficient and popular modes of

transportation. It covers a significant portion of the city, including both the city center and the surrounding suburbs. The trams run from early morning until midnight, with extended services on weekends and public holidays. The network consists of four lines (A, B, C, and D) that intersect at strategic points, making it easy to transfer between lines. Trams are known for their punctuality and frequency, with departures every few minutes during peak hours. They are a convenient option for accessing major tourist attractions, shopping districts, and residential areas within the city.

Buses:
Bordeaux has an extensive bus network that complements the tramway system, providing additional coverage to areas not served by trams. The buses operate from early morning until late at night, with reduced services on Sundays and public holidays. The network consists of several bus lines, denoted by numbers and letters, which connect different neighborhoods and suburbs. Buses are an excellent choice for reaching destinations beyond the tramway routes and exploring the outskirts of Bordeaux. They offer affordable fares and provide a comfortable and reliable means of transportation.

Bicycle:
Bordeaux is a bike-friendly city with a well-developed cycling infrastructure. The city has an efficient bike-sharing system called V^3, which provides bicycles for rent at various docking stations throughout Bordeaux. Renting a bike is a great way to explore the city at your own pace while enjoying the pleasant weather and scenic views. Bordeaux also offers numerous dedicated cycling paths and lanes, making it safe and convenient for cyclists. With its flat terrain, the city is ideal for biking, and it allows you to reach many attractions quickly, avoid traffic congestion, and experience the local culture up close.

Walking:
Bordeaux's city center is relatively compact and easily walkable, making walking a popular mode of transportation for shorter distances. The historic streets, charming squares, and picturesque riverfront make strolling around the city a delightful experience. Many of Bordeaux's major landmarks, such as the Place de la Bourse, the Bordeaux Cathedral, and the Grand Théâtre, are within walking distance of each other. Exploring Bordeaux on foot allows you to appreciate the city's architectural

beauty, discover hidden gems, and immerse yourself in its vibrant atmosphere.

Taxis and Ridesharing:
Taxis are available in Bordeaux and can be hailed on the street or found at designated taxi stands. Taxis are a convenient option for traveling to specific destinations or for those who prefer door-to-door service. Additionally, ridesharing services such as Uber are also available in Bordeaux, providing an alternative means of transportation with the convenience of booking a ride through a mobile app.

River Cruises:
Bordeaux is bisected by the Garonne River, and taking a river cruise is an enchanting way to explore the city and its surrounding areas. Several companies offer guided tours and cruises along the Garonne River, providing a unique perspective of Bordeaux's waterfront and its iconic landmarks. These cruises often include informative commentary about the city's history, architecture, and the region's renowned wine industry. Whether you opt for a short sightseeing cruise or a longer excursion to the vineyards and châteaux in the nearby wine regions, a river cruise offers a memorable and scenic experience.

Car Rental:
For those who prefer the freedom of having their own transportation, renting a car in Bordeaux is a viable option. There are numerous car rental agencies located in the city, including at the Bordeaux-Mérignac Airport. Renting a car allows you to explore Bordeaux and its surrounding regions at your own pace and visit more remote attractions that may not be easily accessible by public transportation. However, it's important to note that driving in the city center can be challenging due to narrow streets, limited parking spaces, and traffic restrictions. It is advisable to familiarize yourself with the local traffic regulations and parking options before embarking on your journey.

Train:
Bordeaux is well-connected to other major cities in France and Europe through its excellent train network. The city's main train station, Gare de Bordeaux-Saint-Jean, is a major transportation hub with high-speed TGV trains that can take you to destinations such as Paris, Lyon, Marseille, and Toulouse. The train is a convenient option for day trips or exploring other regions during your stay in Bordeaux. It

offers comfort, speed, and the opportunity to enjoy the picturesque landscapes of the French countryside.

Tourist Information Centers:
Bordeaux has several tourist information centers located throughout the city, where you can obtain maps, brochures, and helpful advice about getting around. These centers can provide information on public transportation routes, schedules, and ticket prices. They are also a great resource for learning about guided tours, excursions, and special events happening in and around Bordeaux during your visit. The knowledgeable staff can assist you in planning your itinerary and ensuring that you make the most of your time in the city.

In conclusion, getting around Bordeaux is a breeze thanks to its well-connected transportation system. Whether you prefer the efficiency of trams, the flexibility of buses, the freedom of cycling, the leisurely pace of walking, or the convenience of taxis and ridesharing, Bordeaux offers a range of options to suit your needs. By utilizing these modes of transportation, you can navigate the city seamlessly, discover its many attractions, and fully enjoy your time in this remarkable French destination.

Planning Your Trip to Bordeaux

Best Time to Visit Bordeaux

Planning a trip to Bordeaux requires careful consideration of various factors, and one of the most important aspects to consider is the best time to visit. The city experiences a temperate climate, with mild winters and warm summers, but there are certain periods that offer unique experiences and advantages for travelers. In this guide, we will explore the best time to visit Bordeaux based on weather, festivals, and other considerations.

Spring (March to May):
Spring is a delightful time to visit Bordeaux, as the city awakens from its winter slumber. During this period, the weather gradually becomes milder, with temperatures ranging from 10°C (50°F) to 20°C (68°F). The city's parks and gardens come to life with colorful blooms, making it an ideal time for nature enthusiasts. It is also the season when the vineyards begin to blossom, creating a picturesque landscape. However, it's worth noting that spring can be unpredictable, with

35

occasional showers, so packing a light jacket and an umbrella is advisable.

Summer (June to August):
Summer in Bordeaux brings warm and sunny weather, with temperatures averaging between 20°C (68°F) and 30°C (86°F). This is the peak tourist season, as visitors flock to the city to explore its cultural sites, enjoy outdoor activities, and indulge in the world-famous wines. The longer days allow for extended sightseeing and leisurely evenings by the river. However, it's important to note that summer can also be quite busy, and prices for accommodations and flights tend to be higher. Booking in advance is recommended to secure preferred accommodations and avoid any disappointment.

Fall (September to November):
Fall is another excellent time to visit Bordeaux, especially for wine lovers. The vineyards are bustling with activity as the harvest season begins, and visitors have the opportunity to witness the winemaking process firsthand. The temperatures range from 10°C (50°F) to 20°C (68°F), and the city experiences a beautiful array of autumn colors. The crowds thin out compared to the summer months, making it a

more peaceful time to explore Bordeaux's attractions. It's worth considering that rain showers become more frequent during this season, so packing a waterproof jacket or umbrella is advisable.

Winter (December to February):
Winter in Bordeaux is mild compared to many other parts of France, with temperatures ranging from 5°C (41°F) to 12°C (54°F). While the city experiences shorter days and occasional rainfall, it offers a unique charm during this season. Winter is an ideal time to visit for those who prefer fewer crowds and lower prices. Bordeaux's historic buildings and landmarks take on a magical atmosphere, and cozy wine bars provide the perfect setting to indulge in local vintages. It's worth noting that some tourist attractions might have reduced hours or closures during the winter season, so checking ahead is recommended.

In addition to weather considerations, it's worth mentioning some key events and festivals that take place in Bordeaux throughout the year. The Bordeaux Wine Festival in June is a major highlight, showcasing the region's wines and attracting visitors from around the world. The Fête du

Vin Nouveau in November celebrates the arrival of new wines, offering tastings and entertainment. The Christmas market, held during December, transforms the city into a festive wonderland, with stalls selling crafts, food, and gifts.

Ultimately, the best time to visit Bordeaux depends on personal preferences and interests. Whether you choose to explore the city during its vibrant summer months, witness the harvest in the fall, admire the spring blossoms, or experience the cozy winter ambiance, Bordeaux offers something unique and captivating throughout the year.

Duration of Stay

Planning the duration of your stay in Bordeaux is essential to make the most of your trip and immerse yourself in the region's charms. To help you plan your visit effectively, here is a well-written and detailed guide on determining the ideal duration of your stay in Bordeaux.

Consider Your Interests:
The first step in deciding the duration of your trip to Bordeaux is to consider your interests

and the activities you wish to engage in. Bordeaux offers a diverse range of attractions, including wine tasting tours, visits to châteaux, art museums, historical landmarks, and exploring the beautiful countryside. Take some time to create an itinerary based on your preferences to determine the duration required to cover your desired activities.

Wine and Culinary Experiences:
Bordeaux is renowned for its exceptional wines, making it a popular destination for wine enthusiasts. If you plan to delve into the world of Bordeaux wines, you might want to spend at least three to five days in the region. This duration allows you to visit prestigious wine estates, participate in tasting sessions, learn about the winemaking process, and explore the beautiful vineyards of Medoc, Saint-Émilion, or Pessac-Léognan. Additionally, you can indulge in the region's gastronomy by savoring delicious local cuisine at various restaurants and food markets.

City Exploration:
Bordeaux itself offers a vibrant cityscape with a blend of historic and modern attractions. The city is known for its stunning architecture, such as the Place de la Bourse, Grand Théâtre, and

the Gothic-style Bordeaux Cathedral. To explore the city thoroughly and experience its lively ambiance, plan to spend at least two to three days in Bordeaux. This timeframe allows you to visit the main landmarks, stroll along the Garonne River, explore the charming neighborhoods, and discover the local shops, cafés, and markets.

Surrounding Areas:
Beyond the city of Bordeaux, the region boasts captivating landscapes and cultural sites that are worth exploring. If you wish to venture outside the city, you can consider adding an additional two to four days to your itinerary. The nearby Dordogne region, with its prehistoric caves, medieval towns like Sarlat-la-Canéda, and the stunning Lascaux caves, is an excellent choice for history and nature lovers. The coastal town of Arcachon, with its beautiful beaches and the famous Dune du Pilat, is also within easy reach from Bordeaux and can be explored in a day trip or overnight stay.

Total Duration:
Based on the above recommendations, a well-rounded trip to Bordeaux typically requires a minimum of five to seven days. This duration

allows you to experience the city's highlights, immerse yourself in wine and culinary experiences, and explore the surrounding areas. However, if you have more time available, extending your stay by a few days enables you to delve deeper into the region's treasures, enjoy leisurely excursions, or even take day trips to nearby destinations such as the charming villages of Saint-Émilion or the Basque Country.

Remember, the suggested duration is a general guideline, and you can tailor it to suit your preferences and available time. By considering your interests, allocating sufficient time for various activities, and balancing city exploration with day trips, you can plan a memorable and fulfilling trip to Bordeaux.

Budgeting for Your Trip

Bordeaux, located in southwestern France, is a vibrant and culturally rich city renowned for its world-class wines, stunning architecture, and picturesque landscapes. As you embark on planning your trip to Bordeaux, it's essential to establish a well-thought-out budget to ensure you make the most of your experience without breaking the bank. In this guide, we will provide you with a detailed breakdown of the key factors to consider when budgeting for your trip to Bordeaux.

Transportation:

First and foremost, determine how you will be reaching Bordeaux. If you plan to fly, research flight options and compare prices from various airlines to secure the best deal. Bordeaux has its international airport, Merignac Airport, which offers connections to major cities in Europe and beyond.

Once in Bordeaux, consider using public transportation to get around the city and its surrounding areas. Bordeaux has an efficient tram and bus network that can be cost-effective and convenient. A single tram or bus ticket typically costs around €1.60, while day passes are available for approximately €4.50. Taxis and ride-sharing services are also available but can be more expensive.

Accommodation:

Accommodation costs will depend on your preferences and the level of comfort you desire. Bordeaux offers a range of options, including luxury hotels, budget hotels, guesthouses, and hostels. Prices can vary significantly depending on the location and season. As a general guideline, budget travelers can expect to spend around €50-100 per night for a mid-range hotel or guesthouse.

Consider staying in central areas like the historic city center (La Ville de Bordeaux) or the Chartrons district to be close to major attractions, restaurants, and nightlife. Alternatively, if you're on a tighter budget, explore options slightly outside the city center, where prices may be more affordable.

Food and Dining:
Bordeaux is known for its exceptional cuisine, with numerous restaurants and cafes offering a variety of gastronomic delights. While dining out can be a memorable experience, it's important to allocate a reasonable portion of your budget for meals.

To save money, consider having a mix of restaurant meals and self-catered options. Many accommodations provide kitchen facilities, allowing you to prepare simple meals using local ingredients purchased from markets or supermarkets. Additionally, Bordeaux has numerous bakeries and delis where you can pick up affordable and delicious sandwiches or pastries for a quick meal.

A mid-range restaurant meal in Bordeaux can cost between €15-30 per person, excluding drinks. If you're on a tight budget, opt for fixed-price menus (menu du jour) offered at many establishments for a more affordable dining experience.

Sightseeing and Activities:
Bordeaux offers a wealth of sightseeing opportunities, from exploring historic landmarks to visiting renowned wineries and museums. Some attractions have entry fees, so it's important to include these costs in your budget.
Research the attractions you wish to visit and check their admission fees in advance. Many attractions offer discounted rates for students, seniors, or groups, so be sure to inquire about these options. Additionally, consider purchasing a Bordeaux City Pass, which provides free or discounted entry to numerous attractions, along with unlimited public transportation usage.

It's also worth exploring the city's free attractions, such as the beautiful public parks, gardens, and walking tours, which offer a chance to experience Bordeaux's charm without spending extra money.

Wine Tasting:
A visit to Bordeaux wouldn't be complete without indulging in wine tasting experiences. While some wine tours and tastings can be expensive, there are options available to suit different budgets.
Consider visiting wineries located slightly outside the city center, as they often offer more affordable tours and tastings compared to those in the heart of Bordeaux. Alternatively, you can explore the city's wine bars, where you can sample a variety of local wines by the glass or in tasting flights at more reasonable prices.

Miscellaneous Expenses:
Don't forget to factor in miscellaneous expenses such as local transportation within the city, shopping, souvenirs, and unforeseen costs. It's always a good idea to set aside a small contingency fund to cover any unexpected expenses or emergencies that may arise during your trip.

In conclusion, planning your trip to Bordeaux requires careful budgeting to ensure you make the most of your experience without overspending. By considering transportation, accommodation, dining, sightseeing, wine tasting, and miscellaneous expenses, you can create a realistic budget that allows you to explore Bordeaux's rich offerings while staying within your financial means. Remember to research and compare prices in advance, make use of available discounts, and prioritize your spending based on your interests and priorities. Bon voyage!

Accommodation Options

Bordeaux, located in southwestern France, is a vibrant city known for its rich history, beautiful architecture, and world-renowned wine. When planning your trip to Bordeaux, one of the key considerations is finding suitable accommodation that meets your preferences and budget. Bordeaux offers a diverse range of options, from luxury hotels to budget-friendly guesthouses, ensuring there is something to suit every traveler. In this guide, we will explore the various accommodation options available in Bordeaux and provide you with essential information to help you make an informed decision.

Hotels: Bordeaux boasts a wide selection of hotels, ranging from luxurious five-star establishments to more affordable options. The city center, known as the "Golden Triangle," is a popular area to stay due to its proximity to major attractions, shopping areas, and restaurants. You'll find well-known hotel chains like InterContinental, Hilton, and Radisson Blu, offering excellent amenities, comfortable rooms, and attentive service. If you prefer a more intimate experience, boutique hotels can be found in the historic districts, providing unique charm and personalized service.

Guesthouses and Bed and Breakfasts: For a more local and cozy experience, consider staying in a guesthouse or bed and breakfast (B&B). These accommodations often offer a more intimate atmosphere and personalized attention from the hosts. Many guesthouses are situated in residential neighborhoods, allowing you to immerse yourself in the local culture. These establishments typically provide comfortable rooms and serve delicious homemade breakfasts, offering a great value for money.

Apartments and Vacation Rentals: If you prefer more space and independence, renting an apartment or vacation home can be an excellent choice. Bordeaux has numerous rental options available, ranging from stylish apartments in the city center to charming countryside cottages. Renting an apartment allows you to have a more authentic experience, as you can live like a local, shop at neighborhood markets, and prepare your meals. Websites like Airbnb and Vrbo offer a wide range of options to suit various budgets and group sizes.

Chateaux and Vineyard Stays: Bordeaux's wine region is renowned worldwide, and what better way to experience it than by staying in a chateau or vineyard? Many wine estates in the surrounding countryside offer accommodations, allowing you to enjoy the serene beauty of the vineyards and indulge in wine tastings and tours. These properties often provide luxurious rooms, exquisite dining options, and picturesque landscapes. Staying in a chateau or vineyard can be a memorable and unique experience, especially for wine enthusiasts.

Hostels: For budget-conscious travelers or those seeking a more social environment, hostels are a popular choice. Bordeaux has several well-maintained and comfortable hostels, particularly in the city center. These accommodations typically offer dormitory-style rooms with shared facilities, communal spaces for socializing, and often provide organized activities and tours. Hostels are a fantastic option for solo travelers, backpackers, or anyone looking to meet fellow adventurers.

When planning your trip to Bordeaux, consider the following factors when choosing your accommodation:

Location: Decide whether you want to stay in the city center for easy access to attractions or prefer a quieter neighborhood outside the city.
Budget: Determine your budget range and explore options that fit within your financial constraints.
Amenities: Consider the facilities and services offered by each accommodation, such as Wi-Fi, breakfast, parking, and 24-hour reception.

Reviews: Read reviews from previous guests to gauge the quality and reliability of the accommodations.

Accessibility: If you're reliant on public transportation, check the proximity of your accommodation to bus or tram stops.

Special Requirements: If you have specific needs, such as wheelchair accessibility or pet-friendly accommodations, ensure that your chosen option can accommodate them.

In conclusion, Bordeaux offers a wide range of accommodation options to suit every traveler's needs and preferences. Whether you're seeking luxury and indulgence or a budget-friendly stay, you'll find plenty of choices in this charming French city. Take your time to research and consider the various options available, keeping in mind your budget, location preferences, and desired amenities. By planning your accommodation carefully, you can ensure a comfortable and enjoyable stay in Bordeaux.

Comment []: Hotel Bleu de mer

Comment []: Staycity aparthotels Bordeaux City

Exploring Bordeaux City

Bordeaux City Center

Bordeaux, located in southwestern France, is a city renowned for its rich history, stunning architecture, and world-class wine. Bordeaux City Center serves as the heart of this vibrant city and offers a plethora of attractions and activities for visitors to explore. Whether you are a history enthusiast, a wine lover, or simply someone looking to soak up the atmosphere of a charming French city, Bordeaux City Center is sure to captivate you. In this guide, we will delve into the details of what makes Bordeaux City Center a must-visit destination.

Place de la Bourse: One of the most iconic landmarks in Bordeaux, Place de la Bourse is a stunning example of 18th-century architecture. The centerpiece of this square is the Place de la Bourse itself, a magnificent palace built during the reign of Louis XV. The grandeur of the building is enhanced by the Miroir d'eau (Water Mirror), an expansive reflecting pool that creates beautiful mirror-like reflections, making it a popular spot for both locals and tourists.

Cathédrale Saint-André: Situated in the heart of Bordeaux City Center, Cathédrale Saint-André is a masterpiece of Gothic architecture. Construction of this grand cathedral began in the 12th century and continued over the centuries, resulting in a fusion of architectural styles. The intricate carvings, soaring vaulted ceilings, and impressive stained glass windows make it a must-see attraction for history and architecture buffs.

Rue Sainte-Catherine: If you're a fan of shopping, Rue Sainte-Catherine is the place to be. As one of the longest shopping streets in Europe, this bustling pedestrianized street is lined with an array of shops, boutiques, and department stores. From high-end fashion to local specialty stores, you'll find something for every taste and budget. Take a leisurely stroll along this vibrant street, explore the shops, and enjoy the lively atmosphere.

Musée des Beaux-Arts: Art enthusiasts should not miss the Musée des Beaux-Arts in Bordeaux City Center. Housed in a former palace, this museum boasts an impressive collection of artwork spanning from the 16th to the 20th century. From Old Masters to contemporary artists, the museum showcases paintings, sculptures, and decorative arts from renowned artists such as Rubens, Renoir, and Matisse. The beautifully curated exhibits make it a cultural gem worth visiting.

Porte Cailhau: As you wander through the narrow streets of Bordeaux City Center, you will come across the Porte Cailhau, a medieval gate that once served as the main entrance to the city. This historic monument is a testament to Bordeaux's medieval past and provides a glimpse into the city's architectural heritage. Climb to the top of the tower for panoramic views of Bordeaux and the Garonne River, offering a perfect photo opportunity.

Bordeaux Wine Museum: No visit to Bordeaux is complete without indulging in its world-renowned wines. The Bordeaux Wine Museum, located in Bordeaux City Center, offers a comprehensive insight into the region's wine production. Explore the interactive exhibits, learn about the winemaking process, and discover the history and traditions associated with Bordeaux wines. Don't forget to sample some of the exquisite wines at the museum's tasting room.

La Grosse Cloche: Another historic gem in Bordeaux City Center is La Grosse Cloche, a medieval bell tower that dates back to the 15th century. This impressive tower, adorned with intricate carvings, houses a large bell that used to announce curfews and other important events in the city's past. Take a guided tour to learn about its fascinating history and enjoy the panoramic views from the top.

In addition to these highlights, Bordeaux City Center is teeming with charming squares, picturesque streets, and cozy cafes, where you can relax and soak in the vibrant ambiance. The city center is also known for its vibrant food scene, offering a diverse range of culinary delights, from traditional French cuisine to international flavors.

Bordeaux City Center is easily accessible on foot, allowing visitors to immerse themselves in the city's unique atmosphere. So, lace up your walking shoes, grab a map, and get ready to explore the captivating Bordeaux City Center, where history, culture, and exquisite wine come together to create an unforgettable experience.

Place de la Bourse

Bordeaux, located in southwestern France, is known for its rich history, stunning architecture, and world-renowned vineyards. One of the city's most iconic landmarks is the Place de la Bourse, an exquisite square that showcases the grandeur and elegance of Bordeaux. This article will provide you with a detailed overview of Place de la Bourse, highlighting its history, architecture, and the attractions surrounding it.

History:
Place de la Bourse, also known as the Palace Royale, is a neoclassical square situated on the edge of the Garonne River. Construction of this magnificent square began in 1730 and was completed in 1775 under the reign of King

Louis XV. It was designed by the architect Ange-Jacques Gabriel, who aimed to create a symbol of Bordeaux's prosperity and connection to maritime trade.

Architecture:

The architecture of Place de la Bourse is a remarkable blend of elegance, symmetry, and grandeur. At the center of the square stands the famous Fountain of the Three Graces, representing Aglaea, Euphrosyne, and Thalia—daughters of Zeus and symbols of charm, joy, and beauty. The fountain adds a touch of grace and serenity to the square.

The most striking feature of Place de la Bourse is the Palais de la Bourse, the former stock exchange building. This stunning structure, with its Corinthian columns and intricate detailing, dominates the square. The central pavilion of the Palais de la Bourse features a monumental portico adorned with sculptures representing Commerce, Agriculture, and the Garonne River. The Palais de la Bourse now serves as the headquarters of the Bordeaux Chamber of Commerce.

Attractions and Surroundings:

Place de la Bourse is not only a visual delight in itself, but it also offers several attractions and notable sites in its vicinity. Here are a few highlights:

Mirror of Water: Adjacent to the square, you will find the Miroir d'eau, the world's largest reflecting pool. This unique water feature covers an area of 3,450 square meters and creates stunning mirror-like reflections of the Palais de la Bourse. It is a popular spot for locals and tourists to relax, play, and capture beautiful photographs.

Quai de la Douane: Located along the Garonne River, the Quai de la Douane is a picturesque waterfront promenade that offers panoramic views of the river, the Place de la Bourse, and the cityscape. Stroll along the quay, enjoy the fresh air, and take in the breathtaking scenery.

Bordeaux River Cruise: From the nearby Port of the Moon, you can embark on a river cruise that takes you on a scenic journey along the Garonne River. Explore the city from a different perspective and marvel at the architectural wonders that line the riverbanks.

Bordeaux City Centre: The Place de la Bourse serves as a gateway to Bordeaux's vibrant city center. From here, you can explore the historic streets, visit museums, indulge in shopping at the boutiques, and savor the local cuisine in the charming restaurants and cafés.

Conclusion:

Place de la Bourse in Bordeaux is a captivating square that showcases the city's architectural splendor and historical significance. With its stunning Palais de la Bourse, the Fountain of the Three Graces, and the nearby Mirror of Water, it offers a delightful experience for visitors. Whether you're exploring the square, taking a river cruise, or immersing yourself in the vibrant city center, Place de la Bourse is a must-visit destination that encapsulates the charm and allure of Bordeaux.

Cathédrale Saint-André.

Bordeaux, located in southwestern France, is a city renowned for its rich history, stunning architecture, and exquisite wine culture. One of the city's most significant landmarks is the Cathédrale Saint-André, a masterpiece of Gothic architecture. This majestic cathedral stands as a testament to Bordeaux's medieval past and attracts visitors from around the world. In this detailed guide, we will delve into the history, architecture, and notable features of the Cathédrale Saint-André, providing you with all the information you need to explore and appreciate this magnificent monument.

History:

Construction of the Cathédrale Saint-André began in the 12th century and continued over several centuries, resulting in a blend of architectural styles. The cathedral served as the seat of the Archdiocese of Bordeaux and played a significant role in the religious and political life of the region. The original structure was built on the site of an earlier Romanesque church and underwent several modifications and expansions throughout its history.

Architecture:
The Cathédrale Saint-André is a masterpiece of Gothic architecture, characterized by its soaring spires, intricate stone carvings, and breathtaking stained glass windows. The cathedral features a cruciform plan, with a nave, transepts, and an apse. The exterior is adorned with ornate sculptures depicting biblical scenes, saints, and grotesque figures, showcasing the craftsmanship of the medieval artisans.

Notable Features:

Gargoyles and Sculptures: The exterior of the Cathédrale Saint-André is adorned with numerous sculptures, including gargoyles and grotesques. These fascinating stone carvings serve both decorative and functional purposes, channeling rainwater away from the building. Take your time to admire the intricate details and whimsical designs of these sculptures.

Pey-Berland Tower: Adjacent to the cathedral stands the Pey-Berland Tower, a separate bell tower constructed in the 15th century. Visitors can climb the tower's narrow staircase to reach the top and enjoy panoramic views of Bordeaux. The tower's name comes from the archbishop who commissioned its construction, Pey-Berland.

Stained Glass Windows: The Cathédrale Saint-André boasts a stunning collection of stained glass windows, which illuminate the interior with a kaleidoscope of colors. These windows depict various biblical scenes and saints and are a testament to the artistry and skill of medieval glassmakers. The Rose Window, located on the western façade, is particularly noteworthy.

Organ: The cathedral is home to a magnificent organ with over 6,000 pipes. The grand sound of this instrument adds to the spiritual ambiance of the space. If you're lucky, you may have the opportunity to attend a recital or musical performance to experience the organ's majestic tones.

Exploration Tips:

Guided Tours: To fully appreciate the history and architectural significance of the Cathédrale Saint-André, consider joining a guided tour. Knowledgeable guides will provide fascinating insights and anecdotes, enhancing your understanding of this remarkable monument.

Opening Hours and Admission: The cathedral is open to the public, and entry is generally free. However, it is advisable to check the opening hours beforehand, as they may vary. Remember that the cathedral is a place of worship, so be respectful of any ongoing religious ceremonies or services.

Photography: Photography is allowed inside the cathedral, but it is essential to be mindful of other visitors and the sacred nature of the space. Ensure that you follow any specific guidelines provided by the cathedral staff.

Nearby Attractions: The Cathédrale Saint-André is located in the heart of Bordeaux, making it an ideal starting point for exploring the city. Take the time to explore the charming streets, visit the nearby Place de la Bourse, or indulge in some wine tasting at one of the city's renowned wineries.

Conclusion:
The Cathédrale Saint-André in Bordeaux is a remarkable architectural gem, showcasing the city's rich history and religious heritage. From its awe-inspiring façade to its intricate details and stunning stained glass, this cathedral offers a captivating experience for visitors. Take the time to explore its remarkable features, immerse yourself in the peaceful ambiance, and appreciate the timeless beauty of this magnificent structure.

Porte Cailhau

Bordeaux, located in southwestern France, is renowned for its rich history, vibrant culture, and exceptional wine. As you wander through the city, one of the architectural gems that will captivate your attention is the Porte Cailhau. This magnificent gateway stands as a testament to Bordeaux's medieval past and offers visitors a glimpse into the city's architectural heritage. In this guide, we will delve into the history, significance, and highlights of exploring Porte Cailhau in Bordeaux.

History:

Porte Cailhau, also known as the Cailhau Gate, was built during the late 15th century as part of Bordeaux's fortified city walls. Its construction was commissioned by the mayor at the time, Jean de Cailhau, hence the name. The gate was designed as a ceremonial entrance to the city and served both defensive and ornamental purposes.

Architecture:
Porte Cailhau showcases the characteristic architectural style of the late Middle Ages. The gate stands tall, towering over the surrounding area, with its elegant Gothic design. The central archway, flanked by two smaller arches, forms the main entrance. Above the arches, you'll find intricately carved stone decorations, including statues, gargoyles, and floral motifs, all contributing to the gate's grandeur.

Significance:
Beyond its impressive aesthetic appeal, Porte Cailhau holds significant historical and cultural importance. During the Renaissance period, the gate served as a symbol of Bordeaux's prosperity and power. It was through this gateway that important dignitaries and royalty would enter the city, welcomed by grand ceremonies and festivities. Today, Porte

Cailhau remains a prominent landmark and a cherished emblem of Bordeaux's heritage.

Exploring Porte Cailhau:
As you approach Porte Cailhau, you'll be greeted by a square known as Place du Palais. The square offers an ideal vantage point to admire the gate's magnificent facade and take stunning photographs. You can also spend some time absorbing the ambiance of the area and enjoying the bustling atmosphere of Bordeaux.

Upon entering the gate, you'll find yourself in a small museum that provides further insights into the history and construction of Porte Cailhau. The museum showcases artifacts, models, and informative displays, offering visitors a deeper understanding of the gate's significance and the medieval era it represents.

Climbing to the top of Porte Cailhau is a must-do experience. From the upper levels, you'll be rewarded with panoramic views of Bordeaux, including the Garonne River, the historic district, and the surrounding architectural marvels. The vistas are particularly enchanting during sunset, as the fading light casts a warm glow over the cityscape.

Tips for Visiting:

Check the opening hours: Porte Cailhau is typically open to visitors during the day, but it's recommended to check the opening hours in advance to avoid disappointment.

Guided tours: Consider joining a guided tour to gain a deeper understanding of the gate's history and significance. Professional guides can provide valuable insights and anecdotes, enhancing your overall experience.

Combine with other attractions: While exploring Porte Cailhau, take the opportunity to visit other nearby attractions, such as the Bordeaux Cathedral and the Place de la Bourse. These landmarks are within walking distance and will further enrich your visit to Bordeaux.

Conclusion:
Porte Cailhau stands as a magnificent testament to Bordeaux's medieval heritage, beckoning visitors to step back in time and admire its grandeur. From its stunning architectural details to the breathtaking views from the top, exploring Porte Cailhau is a captivating experience that shouldn't be

missed. Immerse yourself in the history, culture, and beauty of Bordeaux, and let this remarkable gateway transport you to a bygone era.

La Cité du Vin

Among the city's many attractions, La Cité du Vin stands out as a must-visit destination for wine enthusiasts and culture lovers alike. La Cité du Vin, meaning "The City of Wine," is a unique cultural center dedicated to the history, culture, and art of wine.

Location and Architecture:
Situated on the banks of the Garonne River in the Bassins à Flot district, La Cité du Vin is an

architectural marvel. Designed by the renowned architects Anouk Legendre and Nicolas Desmazières, the building is inspired by the shape of a wine decanter and features a sleek, contemporary design. Its impressive height of 55 meters and shimmering facade make it a prominent landmark in Bordeaux's skyline.

Exhibitions and Collections:
La Cité du Vin offers a vast range of exhibitions and collections that delve into the world of wine. The permanent exhibition, spread over 3,000 square meters, takes visitors on a multisensory journey through time and space, exploring the history, traditions, and cultural significance of wine. Through interactive displays, audiovisual presentations, and immersive experiences, visitors can learn about various wine-producing regions, grape varieties, winemaking techniques, and the role of wine in different civilizations.

Belvedere and Wine Tasting:
One of the highlights of La Cité du Vin is the Belvedere, an observation deck located on the 8th floor of the building. From this panoramic viewpoint, visitors can enjoy stunning 360-degree views of Bordeaux while sipping on a

glass of wine from one of the world's greatest wine regions. The Belvedere offers a selection of wines from different countries, allowing visitors to indulge in tastings and expand their wine knowledge.

Workshops and Events:
La Cité du Vin organizes a wide array of workshops and events to engage visitors and deepen their understanding of wine culture. These activities cater to all levels of wine enthusiasts, from beginners to connoisseurs. Visitors can participate in wine tasting workshops led by experts, attend masterclasses on specific wine topics, or take part in culinary events that explore the art of food and wine pairing. Additionally, La Cité du Vin hosts temporary exhibitions, conferences, and cultural events related to wine and its broader cultural context.

The Wine Shop and Restaurants:
To complete the experience, La Cité du Vin boasts a comprehensive wine shop where visitors can explore an extensive collection of wines from around the world. Whether you are looking for iconic Bordeaux wines or seeking new discoveries, the shop offers an excellent selection to suit every palate. Moreover, the

complex features two restaurants: Le 7, a panoramic restaurant on the seventh floor with gourmet cuisine and breathtaking views, and Latitude20, a more casual wine bar offering regional delicacies and an extensive wine list.

Practical Information:
La Cité du Vin is easily accessible by public transportation, with tram and bus lines connecting it to various parts of Bordeaux. The center is open daily, and it is advisable to allocate at least half a day to fully explore the exhibitions and enjoy the activities. Admission tickets can be purchased online in advance or directly at the entrance. Additionally, audio guides are available in multiple languages to enhance the visitor experience.

In conclusion, La Cité du Vin in Bordeaux is a remarkable destination that immerses visitors in the world of wine, combining education, entertainment, and cultural enrichment. Whether you are a wine enthusiast, a history buff, or simply seeking a unique experience, this remarkable institution is sure to leave a lasting impression as you explore the fascinating world of wine in the heart of Bordeaux.

Historic Neighborhoods

Bordeaux, located in southwestern France, is a city renowned for its rich history, stunning architecture, and vibrant culture. The city's historic neighborhoods offer visitors a fascinating glimpse into its past, with beautifully preserved buildings, charming streets, and a myriad of cultural attractions. Here, we will delve into some of Bordeaux's most notable historic neighborhoods, showcasing their unique characteristics and must-visit landmarks.

Saint-Pierre: As the oldest district in Bordeaux, Saint-Pierre is a treasure trove of history. Its narrow cobblestone streets wind through a maze of medieval buildings, creating an enchanting atmosphere. The centerpiece of the neighborhood is the magnificent Saint-André Cathedral, a masterpiece of Gothic architecture dating back to the 13th century. Take a leisurely stroll along Rue Sainte-Catherine, the city's main shopping street, and explore the lively Place de la Bourse, an iconic square overlooking the Garonne River.

Chartrons: Located along the banks of the Garonne River, Chartrons is a former wine merchant district that has preserved its distinct character. This neighborhood boasts elegant 18th-century buildings, which were once the homes and warehouses of wealthy wine traders. Today, it is known for its antique shops, art galleries, and trendy boutiques. Don't miss the Musée du Vin et du Négoce, a museum dedicated to Bordeaux's wine trade history, housed in a former wine merchant's residence.

Saint-Michel: Situated on the right bank of the Garonne River, Saint-Michel is a vibrant neighborhood with a bohemian atmosphere. Its focal point is the magnificent Basilica of Saint-Michel, a Gothic masterpiece featuring an impressive bell tower. The area around the basilica is a bustling hub of activity, particularly on Sundays when the popular flea market, Marché des Capucins, takes place. Immerse yourself in the lively atmosphere, indulge in local delicacies, and browse through an array of fresh produce, seafood, and regional specialties.

Saint-Seurin: Known for its Roman heritage, Saint-Seurin is a neighborhood filled with archaeological treasures. The Basilica of Saint-Seurin, a UNESCO World Heritage site, is a prime example of early Christian architecture. It houses a crypt adorned with remarkable sarcophagi and is said to be the final resting place of Saint Fort, an early Christian martyr. The neighborhood's peaceful squares, quaint streets, and charming townhouses contribute to its timeless appeal.

Quartier des Grands Hommes: This elegant neighborhood is synonymous with luxury and sophistication. It features grand boulevards, opulent mansions, high-end boutiques, and gourmet restaurants. Place des Quinconces, one of the largest squares in Europe, is a focal point of the area, adorned with statues and fountains. Take a leisurely stroll along Rue du Palais Gallien and admire the remnants of the ancient Gallo-Roman amphitheater. Don't forget to visit the CAPC Musée d'Art Contemporain, a contemporary art museum housed in a former warehouse.

Exploring Bordeaux's historic neighborhoods is an enriching experience that offers a glimpse into the city's past while immersing visitors in its vibrant present. Whether you're wandering through the medieval streets of Saint-Pierre, admiring the grandeur of Quartier des Grands Hommes, or exploring the Roman heritage of Saint-Seurin, Bordeaux's history comes alive at every corner. So, pack your walking shoes, embrace the charm of the city, and embark on a memorable journey through its historic neighborhoods.

Saint Pierre District

The city of Bordeaux, located in southwestern France, is known for its rich history, stunning architecture, and, of course, its world-renowned wines. Among its many charming districts, the Saint Pierre district stands out as a vibrant and lively area that offers visitors a unique blend of history, culture, and gastronomy. Let's delve into the details of exploring Bordeaux City's Saint Pierre District.

Historical Significance:
The Saint Pierre district is the heart of Bordeaux's historic center and dates back to Roman times. It is characterized by narrow, winding streets, picturesque squares, and beautifully preserved buildings from the medieval and Renaissance periods. As you

stroll through the district, you'll find a fascinating mix of architectural styles, including Gothic, classical, and neoclassical influences.

Place de la Bourse and Miroir d'Eau:

One of the district's most iconic landmarks is the Place de la Bourse, a magnificent square that exemplifies Bordeaux's architectural grandeur. This 18th-century square features stunning neoclassical buildings and a central fountain. Just across from the Place de la Bourse, you'll find the Miroir d'Eau (Water Mirror), a unique shallow pool that reflects the surrounding buildings, creating a mesmerizing visual effect.

Rue Sainte-Catherine:

No visit to the Saint Pierre district would be complete without exploring Rue Sainte-Catherine, one of the longest shopping streets in Europe. This bustling pedestrian street is lined with an array of shops, boutiques, cafes, and restaurants, offering something for everyone. Whether you're looking for fashion, souvenirs, or local delicacies, Rue Sainte-Catherine has it all.

Place du Parlement:

Located in the heart of the district, Place du Parlement is a charming square steeped in history. It takes its name from the nearby Palais Rohan, which now houses the Bordeaux Law Courts. The square is adorned with elegant buildings, including the 18th-century Hôtel des Deux-Ponts and the Palace of the Parliament of Bordeaux. It's a delightful spot to relax, people-watch, and soak up the atmosphere of Bordeaux.

Gastronomic Delights:
The Saint Pierre district is a paradise for food enthusiasts. It is home to numerous bistros, brasseries, and restaurants that serve both traditional and innovative French cuisine. From mouthwatering seafood dishes to delectable pastries and, of course, Bordeaux's world-famous wines, you'll find a diverse range of culinary experiences to indulge in.

Cultural Gems:
For culture lovers, the Saint Pierre district offers several notable attractions. The CAPC Musée d'Art Contemporain, housed in a former warehouse, showcases contemporary art exhibitions and installations. The Saint-Pierre Church, with its imposing Gothic architecture,

is another must-visit landmark that reflects the district's rich religious heritage.

Nightlife:
As the sun sets, the Saint Pierre district comes alive with a vibrant nightlife scene. The district is dotted with trendy bars, cocktail lounges, and wine bars where you can sample a variety of local vintages. Whether you prefer a cozy atmosphere or a lively music-filled venue, there's something for every taste in this district after dark.

In conclusion, exploring Bordeaux City's Saint Pierre district is a delightful experience that offers a captivating blend of history, culture, and gastronomy. From its historic squares and winding streets to its culinary delights and vibrant nightlife, this district is a treasure trove waiting to be discovered by visitors. Immerse yourself in the charm and allure of the Saint Pierre district and create lasting memories of your time in Bordeaux.

Saint-Michel District

The city of Bordeaux in southwestern France is known for its rich history, stunning architecture, and world-class wine. One of its most vibrant and eclectic neighborhoods is the Saint-Michel district. Situated on the left bank of the Garonne River, this neighborhood is a cultural and social hub, offering visitors a diverse range of attractions and experiences. In this guide, we will delve into the fascinating aspects of exploring Bordeaux's Saint-Michel district.

Historical Background:
The Saint-Michel district has a long and storied history that dates back to Roman times. It was originally a separate village known as "Saint-Michel de Bordeaux" before being incorporated into the city. Over the centuries, it has evolved into a melting pot of cultures, attracting people from various backgrounds.

Exploring the Architecture:
One of the highlights of the Saint-Michel district is its impressive architecture. The most iconic landmark is the Basilica of Saint-Michel, a stunning Gothic church dating back to the 14th century. Its towering spire and intricate stonework make it a must-visit for architecture

enthusiasts. The nearby Saint-Michel market hall, built in the 19th century, is another architectural gem that showcases the city's vibrant market culture.

Cultural Attractions:
Saint-Michel is known for its vibrant cultural scene. The neighborhood is home to numerous art galleries, theaters, and music venues. The Théâtre des Salinières, a historic theater established in 1783, hosts a variety of performances, including plays, comedy shows, and concerts. The area also houses the CAPC Museum of Contemporary Art, which exhibits a diverse collection of contemporary artworks.

Local Markets and Gastronomy:
The Saint-Michel district is a food lover's paradise. Its bustling markets offer a wide array of fresh produce, regional specialties, and international flavors. The Marché des Capucins, the largest covered market in Bordeaux, is a must-visit. Here, you can sample local delicacies such as canelés (small, caramelized cakes) and enjoy a traditional French breakfast at one of the charming cafes.

Street Art:

Saint-Michel is renowned for its vibrant street art scene. As you wander through its narrow streets and alleyways, you'll come across colorful murals and graffiti that reflect the neighborhood's bohemian spirit. Artists from all over the world contribute to the ever-changing urban art landscape, making it a feast for the eyes and a testament to Bordeaux's thriving artistic community.

Multicultural Vibes:
The Saint-Michel district is a melting pot of cultures, attracting residents and visitors from diverse backgrounds. It has a strong immigrant community that has enriched the neighborhood with its customs, cuisine, and traditions. Exploring the area allows you to experience this multicultural vibrancy, whether through the aromas of international cuisines or the lively atmosphere of its streets.

Nightlife:
When the sun sets, Saint-Michel comes alive with a vibrant nightlife. The district boasts numerous bars, pubs, and clubs that cater to all tastes. From trendy cocktail lounges to lively music venues, there's something for everyone. The streets are often bustling with locals and tourists enjoying the lively atmosphere,

creating a memorable experience for those seeking a night out on the town.

Getting Around:
Saint-Michel is conveniently located within walking distance of Bordeaux's city center. It is easily accessible by public transportation, including tram lines A and C. Exploring the neighborhood on foot is highly recommended, as it allows you to fully immerse yourself in its vibrant ambiance and discover hidden gems along the way.

In conclusion, exploring Bordeaux's Saint-Michel district is a captivating experience that offers a blend of history, culture, gastronomy, and nightlife. From its impressive architecture and cultural attractions to its bustling markets and vibrant street art scene, this neighborhood has something for everyone. Whether you're a history enthusiast, art lover, or foodie, a visit to Saint-Michel is sure to leave you with lasting memories of Bordeaux's rich cultural heritage.

Chartrons District

Located in the heart of Bordeaux, France, the Chartrons district is a vibrant and historic neighborhood that offers a unique blend of culture, history, and gastronomy. Known for its picturesque streets, charming squares, and lively atmosphere, Chartrons is a must-visit destination for anyone exploring the beautiful city of Bordeaux. Let's delve into the details and discover what makes the Chartrons district so special.

History and Architecture:
Chartrons district has a rich history that dates back to the 18th century. It was originally an independent town, home to wine merchants and traders who played a significant role in Bordeaux's booming wine industry. Today, the district still retains its distinct character and charm. The architecture in Chartrons is a blend of styles, ranging from classic 18th-century townhouses to more modern and eclectic designs. As you wander through its streets, you'll come across elegant facades, ornate balconies, and hidden courtyards that evoke the area's history and heritage.

Wine Culture and Trade:

One of the main highlights of Chartrons is its deep connection to Bordeaux's wine culture and trade. Historically, the district was a hub for wine storage, with its proximity to the Garonne River facilitating easy transportation of wine barrels. Many of the old wine warehouses, known as "chais," have been converted into wine shops, cellars, and tasting rooms, providing an opportunity to explore and sample the region's world-renowned wines. Whether you're a wine connoisseur or simply curious about Bordeaux's wine heritage, Chartrons offers a fantastic opportunity to immerse yourself in this cultural aspect.

Quai des Chartrons:
Running alongside the Garonne River, Quai des Chartrons is a picturesque promenade that offers stunning views of the water and the Pont de Pierre bridge. The quay is lined with elegant buildings and is a great place for a leisurely stroll or a relaxing picnic. On Sundays, you can explore the lively Marché des Quais, an open-air market where you can find a variety of fresh produce, local products, crafts, and antiques. It's a wonderful way to experience the local lifestyle and immerse yourself in the vibrant atmosphere of Chartrons.

Musée du Vin et du Négoce:
For those interested in delving deeper into Bordeaux's wine history, a visit to the Musée du Vin et du Négoce is a must. Housed in an 18th-century building, this museum provides an immersive experience into the world of wine production and trade. You can learn about the winemaking process, explore the evolution of wine trade in Bordeaux, and even participate in wine tastings. The museum showcases a fascinating collection of artifacts, including ancient winemaking tools, cooperage workshops, and vintage bottles, offering a comprehensive understanding of Bordeaux's wine heritage.

Gastronomy and Culinary Delights:
Chartrons district is also a haven for food enthusiasts. Along its streets, you'll find a myriad of restaurants, bistros, and cafés serving both traditional French cuisine and innovative culinary creations. From cozy neighborhood brasseries to Michelin-starred establishments, there's something to suit every palate. Additionally, the district hosts numerous food markets, such as the famous Marché des Capucins, where you can sample local delicacies, purchase fresh ingredients, and get a taste of the region's gastronomic delights.

In conclusion, the Chartrons district in Bordeaux offers a captivating blend of history, wine culture, stunning architecture, and culinary experiences. Whether you're exploring the wine cellars, strolling along the quayside, visiting the museum, or indulging in the local cuisine, Chartrons provides a unique and enriching experience for visitors. Immerse yourself in the charm of this vibrant neighborhood and discover the essence of Bordeaux's cultural heritage.

Museums and Galleries

Bordeaux, located in southwestern France, is a city renowned for its rich history, vibrant culture, and world-class wines. In addition to its famous vineyards, Bordeaux also boasts a remarkable collection of museums and galleries that offer visitors a fascinating glimpse into the city's past and present. Whether you're an art enthusiast, history buff, or simply curious about the local heritage, Bordeaux's museums and galleries are sure to captivate your imagination. Let's embark on a virtual tour of some of the must-visit cultural institutions in Bordeaux.

Musée d'Aquitaine:
The Musée d'Aquitaine is a must-visit for those interested in the history and archaeology of the region. The museum showcases a vast collection spanning prehistoric times to the present day, with exhibits focusing on the rich heritage of Aquitaine. You can explore artifacts, ancient artworks, and interactive displays that shed light on the cultural, social, and economic evolution of the region.

Musée des Beaux-Arts:
Housed in a stunning 18th-century building, the Musée des Beaux-Arts is one of the largest fine arts museums in France. The museum showcases an extensive collection of European paintings and sculptures, including works by renowned artists such as Rubens, Delacroix, and Matisse. From the Renaissance to contemporary art, the museum offers a comprehensive overview of Western artistic traditions.

CAPC Musée d'Art Contemporain:
For contemporary art enthusiasts, the CAPC Musée d'Art Contemporain is a must-visit

destination. Located in a former warehouse, this museum hosts a diverse range of temporary exhibitions that push boundaries and challenge conventional artistic norms. From installations and video art to experimental works, the museum provides a platform for emerging and established contemporary artists.

La Cité du Vin:
While not strictly a museum or gallery, La Cité du Vin is a unique cultural institution dedicated to the history, culture, and diversity of wine. It offers a multisensory journey through the world of wine, combining interactive exhibits, immersive displays, and tasting experiences. Visitors can explore the different wine regions of the world, learn about winemaking techniques, and discover the role of wine in various cultures.

Musée du Vin et du Négoce:
Bordeaux's history as a renowned wine-producing region comes to life at the Musée du Vin et du Négoce. Situated in a former wine merchant's house, the museum offers insights into the wine trade and the traditional methods used in winemaking. You can explore the cellars, see the tools and equipment used by

winemakers in the past, and learn about the evolution of Bordeaux wines over the centuries.

Musée National des Douanes:
For a unique museum experience, head to the Musée National des Douanes, dedicated to the history of customs and excise duties. Housed in a magnificent 18th-century building, the museum takes you on a journey through the intriguing world of customs, smuggling, and international trade. You can discover the various roles played by customs officers, explore their historical uniforms and equipment, and learn about the impact of customs on society.

Musée Mer Marine:
Scheduled to open in 2023, the Musée Mer Marine promises to be a captivating museum dedicated to maritime history and exploration. Located in a renovated 19th-century warehouse on the banks of the Garonne River, the museum will showcase an impressive collection of ship models, navigational instruments, and artifacts from maritime expeditions. It aims to provide visitors with a deeper understanding of Bordeaux's maritime heritage and its connections to the wider world.

When exploring Bordeaux's museums and galleries, it's worth checking their opening hours . Many museums offer guided tours, audio guides, or interactive apps to enhance the visitor experience. So, immerse yourself in the rich cultural tapestry of Bordeaux and enjoy the treasure trove of art, history, and heritage that the city has to offer.

Musée d'Aquitaine

The Musée d'Aquitaine, located in the heart of Bordeaux city in southwestern France, is a renowned museum that offers a fascinating glimpse into the rich history and cultural heritage of the Aquitaine region. With its extensive collection spanning prehistoric times to the present day, the museum provides visitors with a comprehensive understanding of the area's past and its significance in shaping France's history.

Established in 1987, the Musée d'Aquitaine is housed in a historic building, the former Palais de l'Archévêché, which dates back to the 18th century. The museum's architecture itself is a sight to behold, with its grand facade and elegant interiors that have been meticulously restored to showcase the exhibits in a fitting setting.

One of the main highlights of the Musée d'Aquitaine is its collection of archaeological artifacts, which trace the region's history from prehistoric times to the Roman era. Visitors can explore an array of ancient objects, including tools, pottery, and sculptures, providing insights into the daily life and customs of the earliest inhabitants of Aquitaine.

Moving forward in history, the museum offers a comprehensive display of the Middle Ages, where visitors can delve into the rich medieval heritage of the region. Intriguing artifacts such as medieval manuscripts, religious objects, and weaponry shed light on the socio-political dynamics and cultural developments during this period.

The museum also boasts an impressive collection that covers the colonial period of Aquitaine. This includes artifacts from the French colonization of North America, particularly the significant role played by the region in the establishment of New France. Visitors can explore the historical context of the region's involvement in transatlantic trade, maritime exploration, and the slave trade.

Moreover, the Musée d'Aquitaine presents an extensive exhibition on the modern history of Bordeaux and the Aquitaine region. This section highlights key events such as the French Revolution, the industrialization of Bordeaux, and the impact of World War II on the city and its residents. Through photographs, documents, and multimedia presentations, visitors can gain a deeper understanding of the city's evolution over time.

To enhance the visitor experience, the museum provides informative displays in both French and English, making it accessible to a wide range of audiences. Additionally, guided tours and audio guides are available for those who seek a more in-depth exploration of the exhibits.

Beyond the permanent collections, the Musée d'Aquitaine also hosts temporary exhibitions that showcase various aspects of regional and international history, art, and culture. These temporary displays ensure that there is always something new and engaging to discover during each visit to the museum.

For those interested in further research or studying specific aspects of Aquitaine's history, the museum houses a specialized library and documentation center. These resources are open to the public and offer a wealth of knowledge for academics, students, and enthusiasts.

In conclusion, a visit to the Musée d'Aquitaine in Bordeaux City provides a captivating journey through the history of the Aquitaine region. From its prehistoric roots to its modern-day significance, the museum offers a comprehensive and engaging exploration of the area's past. Whether you are a history buff, a culture enthusiast, or simply curious about the heritage of Bordeaux and Aquitaine, this museum is a must-visit destination that will leave you with a deeper appreciation for the region's rich historical legacy.

CAPC Musée d'Art Contemporain

Bordeaux, located in southwestern France, is a vibrant city known for its rich cultural heritage, historic architecture, and excellent wine. Among its numerous attractions, the CAPC Musée d'Art Contemporain stands out as a must-visit destination for art enthusiasts. This renowned contemporary art museum offers a fascinating blend of modern artworks, thought-provoking exhibitions, and a unique architectural setting. In this detailed guide, we will delve into the captivating world of CAPC Musée d'Art Contemporain, providing you with all the essential information you need for an enriching visit.

History and Background:
The CAPC Musée d'Art Contemporain, which stands for Contemporary Art Museum of Bordeaux, is situated in a former warehouse, known as Entrepôt Lainé, along the Garonne River. The museum was established in 1973 with the aim of promoting and showcasing contemporary art to the public. It was one of the first contemporary art museums in France and quickly gained recognition for its innovative exhibitions and commitment to emerging artists.

The Building and Architecture:
The museum's location in the Entrepôt Lainé, a 19th-century warehouse, adds to its allure. The architectural transformation of the warehouse into a museum was carried out by the renowned architects Jean-François Bodin, François Fontès, and Bernard Vaudeville. They

successfully combined the historic industrial character of the building with contemporary design elements, creating a harmonious space for artistic expression.

Exhibitions and Collections:
CAPC Musée d'Art Contemporain features a diverse range of contemporary artworks, including installations, sculptures, paintings, photography, and multimedia presentations. The museum's permanent collection comprises over 1,300 artworks, representing various artistic movements and periods from the 1960s to the present day. It includes works by internationally acclaimed artists such as Andy Warhol, Nan Goldin, Anish Kapoor, and Christian Boltanski, among others.

In addition to its permanent collection, the museum regularly hosts temporary exhibitions that explore different themes, artistic concepts, and cultural phenomena. These exhibitions often provide a platform for emerging artists and reflect the ever-changing landscape of contemporary art. The museum's curatorial team ensures a thought-provoking and engaging experience for visitors, fostering dialogue and critical thinking.

Museum Facilities and Amenities:
CAPC Musée d'Art Contemporain offers a range of facilities and amenities to enhance visitors' experience. The museum has a well-curated bookstore where you can find a wide selection of art books, catalogs, and publications. The bookstore also stocks unique and artistic objects, making it an excellent place to find a memorable souvenir.

The museum's on-site café provides a cozy and relaxed environment for visitors to take a break and enjoy a light meal or a cup of coffee. The café often incorporates art-inspired elements into its decor, further immersing visitors in the artistic ambiance of the museum.

Educational Programs and Events:
CAPC Musée d'Art Contemporain is committed to education and outreach. The museum organizes a range of educational programs, including guided tours, workshops, lectures, and artist talks. These activities offer visitors the opportunity to deepen their understanding of contemporary art and engage in meaningful discussions. The museum also collaborates with local schools and universities, providing educational resources and fostering artistic development among the youth.

Additionally, CAPC Musée d'Art Contemporain hosts special events, such as film screenings, performances, and live music, creating a dynamic cultural hub within Bordeaux. These events attract a diverse audience and contribute to the city's vibrant arts scene.

Visiting Information:
To make the most of your visit to CAPC Musée d'Art Contemporain, here are some practical details:

Location: The museum is located at 7 Rue Ferrère, 33000 Bordeaux, France.
Opening Hours: CAPC Musée d'Art Contemporain is open from Tuesday to Sunday, from 11 am to 6 pm.
Admission Fees: General admission is €7, with reduced rates available for students, seniors, and groups. Entry is free for visitors under 18 and on the first Sunday of each month.
Accessibility: The museum is wheelchair accessible, with ramps and elevators available for ease of movement. Large print guides and audio guides are also available for visually impaired visitors.
Transportation: The museum is well-connected by public transportation. Tram lines B and C

have stops nearby, and there are several bus stops within walking distance.

Visitor Guidelines: To ensure a pleasant experience for all, the museum kindly requests visitors to refrain from using flash photography, touching the artworks, and consuming food and drinks within the exhibition areas.

Conclusion:

CAPC Musée d'Art Contemporain in Bordeaux offers an enriching and immersive experience for art enthusiasts and curious visitors alike. With its exceptional collection, thought-provoking exhibitions, and stunning architectural setting, the museum stands as a testament to Bordeaux's commitment to contemporary art. Whether you're a seasoned art connoisseur or simply curious about the world of modern art, a visit to CAPC Musée d'Art Contemporain is sure to leave a lasting impression.

Musée du Vin et du Négoce

Bordeaux, located in southwestern France, is renowned worldwide for its rich history in wine production. As a city deeply connected to viticulture, it is home to numerous wine-related attractions, including the Musée du Vin et du Négoce (Museum of Wine and Trade). This museum provides visitors with a captivating journey through the region's wine heritage, offering insights into the art of winemaking, the history of Bordeaux's wine trade, and the unique terroir that contributes to the creation of exceptional wines. In this detailed information guide, we will delve into the highlights of the Musée du Vin et du Négoce and what visitors can expect from their visit.

Location and History:
The Musée du Vin et du Négoce is situated in the heart of Bordeaux, within the historic district known as Chartrons. Chartrons was historically the center of the city's wine trade, bustling with merchants, warehouses, and shipping activity. This strategic location allows visitors to immerse themselves in the very heart of Bordeaux's wine history.

Exhibits and Collections:
The museum's exhibits are divided into several sections, each providing a unique perspective on Bordeaux's wine industry. Here are some of the key highlights:

History of Wine Trade: This section focuses on the evolution of the Bordeaux wine trade over the centuries. Visitors can explore the origins of the city's commercial success, learning about the key figures, techniques, and navigational routes that shaped the wine industry.

Wine Production Process: One of the main attractions of the museum is its detailed exploration of the winemaking process. Through informative displays and interactive exhibits, visitors gain insights into vine cultivation, grape varieties, fermentation, aging, and bottling. The museum showcases the tools and machinery used throughout history, highlighting the advancements in winemaking techniques.

Wine Tasting and Aromas: To enhance the visitor experience, the museum offers a dedicated space for wine tasting. Here, visitors can sample a selection of Bordeaux wines, guided by knowledgeable staff who provide information on the region's different grape varietals, appellations, and flavor profiles. This sensory journey allows visitors to appreciate the nuances of Bordeaux's world-class wines.

Art and Wine: The Musée du Vin et du Négoce also celebrates the intersection of art and wine. It showcases various artistic representations of wine through paintings, sculptures, and photographs. These artistic pieces provide a deeper appreciation for the cultural significance of wine in Bordeaux's history and its influence on the arts.

Guided Tours and Workshops:
The museum offers guided tours conducted by expert guides who share their extensive knowledge of Bordeaux's wine heritage. These

tours provide a comprehensive overview of the museum's exhibits, ensuring visitors make the most of their visit. Additionally, the museum organizes workshops and educational programs that delve deeper into specific aspects of winemaking, such as blending workshops or vineyard visits, allowing participants to engage in hands-on experiences.

Practical Information:
Here are some practical details to consider when planning your visit to the Musée du Vin et du Négoce:

Opening Hours: The museum is typically open from Tuesday to Sunday, with varying hours. It is advisable to check the official website or contact the museum for the most up-to-date information on opening hours.

Admission Fees: The museum operates on a ticketed entry system, and prices may vary depending on the season and specific exhibitions. Reduced fares are often available for students, seniors, and groups.

Accessibility: The museum is designed to be accessible to visitors with mobility challenges, offering facilities such as wheelchair access and elevators.

Additional Facilities: The Musée du Vin et du Négoce features a gift shop where visitors can purchase wines, books, and other wine-related souvenirs. There may also be a café or restaurant on-site, providing an opportunity to indulge in regional cuisine paired with Bordeaux wines.

Conclusion:

For wine enthusiasts, history buffs, or those simply intrigued by the world of Bordeaux wines, a visit to the Musée du Vin et du Négoce is a must. Through its engaging exhibits, interactive experiences, and knowledgeable guides, the museum offers a comprehensive understanding of Bordeaux's wine culture, from its historic trading roots to the intricacies of winemaking. Exploring this museum provides a fascinating glimpse into the traditions, craftsmanship, and passion that have made Bordeaux one of the most celebrated wine regions in the world.

Parks and Gardens

Beyond its charming streets and iconic landmarks, Bordeaux is also home to a variety of beautiful parks and gardens that offer a tranquil escape from the bustling city life. In this guide, we will explore some of the top parks and gardens in Bordeaux, highlighting their unique features and attractions.

Jardin Public:
Located in the heart of Bordeaux, Jardin Public is one of the city's most beloved parks. Designed in the 18th century, this 11-hectare green oasis offers a perfect blend of natural beauty and man-made elegance. The park is characterized by its symmetrical layout, tree-lined alleys, and a central pond where visitors can rent small boats. Jardin Public is also home to the Natural History Museum, which houses a fascinating collection of exhibits showcasing the region's flora and fauna.

Parc Bordelais:
Spread across 28 hectares in the Caudéran district, Parc Bordelais is a popular destination for both locals and tourists. This vast green space features a variety of activities and amenities, making it an ideal spot for families and outdoor enthusiasts. The park boasts

beautiful English-style gardens, wide open lawns perfect for picnics, a large playground for children, and even a mini-golf course. Visitors can also explore the park's charming rose garden, fountains, and the Théâtre de Verdure, an outdoor theater that hosts cultural events during the summer months.

Jardin Botanique:

Situated near the River Garonne, the Jardin Botanique (Botanical Garden) of Bordeaux offers a peaceful retreat for nature lovers. Spanning over 4.5 hectares, the garden showcases a diverse collection of plant species from around the world. Visitors can meander through themed gardens, such as the Japanese garden with its tranquil pond and bonsai trees, or the aromatic garden filled with fragrant herbs and flowers. The garden also features a tropical greenhouse, an arboretum, and a sensory garden designed to engage all five senses.

Parc Palmer:

Located in the suburb of Cenon, just a short tram ride from Bordeaux's city center, Parc Palmer is a hidden gem awaiting discovery. This expansive park spans over 16 hectares and offers stunning panoramic views of Bordeaux's skyline. Parc Palmer is known for its rolling hills, shady paths, and a large lake where visitors can rent paddleboats. The park also hosts regular events and concerts, providing a lively atmosphere for both locals and visitors.

Parc Majolan:
Situated in the nearby town of Blanquefort, Parc Majolan is a picturesque park that showcases the charm of the Bordeaux region's countryside. This 23-hectare park features beautifully manicured gardens, a lake with elegant swans, and a magnificent château that serves as a backdrop for the scenic landscape. Visitors can explore the park's network of walking trails, admire the vibrant flowerbeds, and relax in peaceful surroundings. Parc Majolan also offers activities such as mini-golf, a zip-line course, and a small train that takes visitors on a tour of the park.

Parc Floral:
Situated in the Chartrons district, Parc Floral is a haven of tranquility known for its stunning display of flowers and plants. This meticulously maintained garden spans over 33 acres and offers a wide range of floral species, including roses, irises, and dahlias. Visitors can wander along the winding pathways, relax on benches

surrounded by colorful blooms, and enjoy the peaceful ambiance. Parc Floral also hosts seasonal events, such as flower shows and horticultural exhibitions, providing visitors with a unique opportunity to appreciate the beauty of nature.

Parc Rivière:

Nestled between the Garonne River and the Bordeaux-Lac neighborhood, Parc Rivière offers a picturesque setting for nature enthusiasts and sports lovers alike. This vast green space encompasses 30 hectares of grassy meadows, woodlands, and walking trails. The park features several sports facilities, including tennis courts, soccer fields, and a skate park, catering to active visitors. Parc Rivière also offers a serene lake where visitors can enjoy fishing or simply relax by the water's edge. With its stunning views of the river and ample space for outdoor activities, the park provides a perfect retreat for recreation and relaxation.

Jardin de l'Hôtel de Ville:

Situated behind the Bordeaux City Hall, Jardin de l'Hôtel de Ville is a charming and intimate garden that offers respite in the city center. This small yet well-maintained park features neatly manicured lawns, flower beds, and a central fountain surrounded by benches. The garden provides a peaceful escape from the bustling streets, making it an ideal spot for a quiet break or a leisurely stroll. Its proximity to other major attractions in Bordeaux also makes it a convenient stop for visitors exploring the city's landmarks.

Parc de l'Ermitage:
Located in the suburb of Lormont, just across the Garonne River from Bordeaux, Parc de l'Ermitage offers a unique blend of natural beauty and historical significance. This park is set on a hill and provides panoramic views of Bordeaux's skyline. Visitors can explore the park's lush greenery, relax in shaded areas, and admire the remains of a 17th-century hermitage, which adds a touch of historical charm to the surroundings. Parc de l'Ermitage is also a popular spot for outdoor concerts and cultural events during the summer months.

Parc Floral du Bourgailh:
Situated in the neighboring town of Pessac, the Parc Floral du Bourgailh is a must-visit destination for nature lovers and garden enthusiasts. Spanning over 100 hectares, this expansive park offers a diverse range of landscapes, including forests, meadows, and

wetlands. Visitors can explore the park's numerous walking trails, discover hidden ponds and waterfalls, and admire the extensive collection of plant species in the botanical garden. The park also features an ecological education center, providing interactive exhibits and workshops on environmental conservation and sustainable practices.

When exploring Bordeaux's parks and gardens, it's essential to respect the natural environment and follow any rules or regulations set by the authorities. Whether you're seeking a tranquil stroll, a family outing, or a peaceful spot to read a book, Bordeaux's parks and gardens provide a delightful setting to connect with nature and unwind in the midst of this vibrant city.

Wine Tourism in Bordeaux

Bordeaux Wine Regions

Wine tourism in Bordeaux is an exquisite experience that combines the appreciation of fine wines with the exploration of breathtaking landscapes, rich history, and cultural heritage. Bordeaux, located in the southwest of France, is one of the most renowned wine regions in the world, producing exceptional wines that have captivated connoisseurs for centuries. With its diverse vineyards, prestigious châteaux, and charming countryside, Bordeaux offers a wine tourism destination like no other.

Bordeaux is home to several distinct wine regions, each with its unique characteristics and terroir, contributing to the exceptional variety and quality of its wines. The main wine regions in Bordeaux include Médoc, Saint-Émilion, Pomerol, Graves, and Sauternes.

Médoc: Situated on the left bank of the Gironde estuary, the Médoc region is famous for its prestigious red wines, particularly

Cabernet Sauvignon blends. Wine lovers can explore the famed appellations of Pauillac, Saint-Julien, Margaux, and Saint-Estèphe, which are home to some of the world's most renowned châteaux, such as Château Lafite Rothschild and Château Margaux.

Saint-Émilion: Located on the right bank of the Dordogne River, the Saint-Émilion region boasts a rich winemaking history dating back to Roman times. The region produces primarily Merlot-based wines known for their elegance and finesse. Visitors can wander through the charming village of Saint-Émilion, a UNESCO World Heritage site, and explore its underground cellars and numerous wineries, including Château Ausone and Château Cheval Blanc.

Pomerol: Adjacent to Saint-Émilion, the Pomerol region is renowned for its powerful and opulent wines, predominantly made from Merlot grapes. Pomerol is home to the iconic Château Pétrus, as well as other esteemed estates like Château Lafleur and Château Le Pin. Wine enthusiasts can savor these unique wines and witness the intimate winemaking practices that have made Pomerol famous.

Graves: Situated on the left bank of the Garonne River, the Graves region produces both red and white wines. The red wines are typically crafted from Cabernet Sauvignon and Merlot, while the whites are primarily made from Sauvignon Blanc and Sémillon. Graves is known for its esteemed appellations of Pessac-Léognan and Sauternes. Visitors can enjoy tastings at renowned châteaux like Château Haut-Brion and Château Pape Clément.

Sauternes: Located within the Graves region, Sauternes is famous for its luscious, golden-hued sweet wines. Produced from noble rot-affected grapes, primarily Sémillon, Sauvignon Blanc, and Muscadelle, Sauternes wines exhibit complex flavors of honey, apricot, and botrytis. Iconic châteaux in Sauternes include Château d'Yquem, Château Suduiraut, and Château Rieussec.

When visiting Bordeaux for wine tourism, there are various activities and experiences to indulge in. Wine enthusiasts can embark on vineyard tours, exploring the picturesque landscapes and learning about the unique terroir that shapes Bordeaux wines. Many châteaux offer guided tours, where visitors can witness the winemaking process, from vine to bottle, and gain insight into the meticulous craftsmanship behind these exceptional wines.

Tastings are a highlight of any wine tourism experience in Bordeaux. Visitors can sample a wide range of wines, from prestigious grand crus to hidden gems, gaining an appreciation for the diverse styles and flavors of Bordeaux. Some châteaux offer personalized tastings and food pairings, allowing guests to savor the wines alongside delectable local cuisine.

To further enhance the wine tourism experience, Bordeaux also offers wine schools and workshops, where visitors can deepen their knowledge of wine production, grape varieties, and wine tasting techniques. These educational opportunities provide a deeper understanding of Bordeaux wines and enable visitors to become true wine connoisseurs.

In addition to the wine-related activities, Bordeaux boasts a rich cultural heritage and historic sites worth exploring. The city of Bordeaux itself is a UNESCO World Heritage site, with stunning architecture, vibrant markets, and gourmet restaurants. Visitors can also discover the region's prehistoric caves, medieval castles, and charming villages, immersing themselves in the local culture and history.

To conclude, wine tourism in Bordeaux offers an unparalleled experience for wine enthusiasts and travelers alike. From the world-renowned vineyards to the historic châteaux and the breathtaking landscapes, Bordeaux's wine regions provide a captivating journey through the art and science of winemaking. Whether it's savoring the finest wines, learning about the winemaking process, or immersing oneself in the region's cultural heritage, Bordeaux offers an unforgettable wine tourism destination.

Wine Tasting and Tours

Bordeaux is a renowned wine region in southwestern France, famous for its exceptional vineyards, prestigious wineries, and rich wine-making heritage. Wine tourism in Bordeaux offers visitors a unique opportunity to explore the picturesque vineyards, indulge in wine tastings, and learn about the region's winemaking traditions. In this guide, we will delve into the world of wine tourism in Bordeaux, focusing on wine tasting and tours.

Bordeaux Wine Region:

Bordeaux is one of the most revered wine regions globally, known for producing some of the finest wines in the world. The region boasts a favorable climate, diverse terroir, and centuries of winemaking expertise. Bordeaux is divided into several sub-regions, each with its distinct characteristics, including Médoc, Saint-Émilion, Pomerol, Graves, and Sauternes, among others. Each sub-region offers unique wine experiences and tasting opportunities.

Wine Tastings:

Wine tastings are an essential part of Bordeaux wine tourism. Numerous châteaux and wineries throughout the region welcome visitors to sample their wines, learn about the winemaking process, and experience the nuances of Bordeaux's diverse wine offerings. Tastings can range from informal sessions at local wine bars to guided tastings at prestigious châteaux. Visitors can savor a wide variety of

Bordeaux wines, including reds, whites, rosés, and sweet wines like Sauternes.

Château Visits and Tours:
Exploring the grand châteaux of Bordeaux is a highlight of wine tourism in the region. Many wineries open their doors to visitors, providing guided tours of their vineyards, cellars, and production facilities. These tours often offer insights into the history, viticulture techniques, and winemaking processes specific to each estate. Visitors can witness the barrel aging process, learn about grape varieties, and gain an understanding of the factors that contribute to Bordeaux's world-renowned wines.

Wine Education:
For those seeking a deeper understanding of Bordeaux wines, wine education programs are available throughout the region. These programs offer comprehensive courses and workshops on various aspects of wine, including grape varietals, wine tasting techniques, food and wine pairings, and the art of blending. Whether you are a wine enthusiast or a professional in the industry, these educational opportunities allow you to expand your knowledge and appreciation of Bordeaux wines.

Wine Festivals and Events:

Bordeaux hosts several wine festivals and events throughout the year, providing a vibrant and festive atmosphere for wine lovers. The Bordeaux Wine Festival, held every two years, is a highlight, attracting thousands of visitors from around the world. This four-day celebration features wine tastings, gourmet food pairings, concerts, art exhibitions, and fireworks, all in the heart of Bordeaux. Other notable events include the Saint-Émilion Wine Festival and the Médoc Marathon, which combines wine tasting and running through the vineyards.

Wine Routes and Itineraries:

Bordeaux offers several wine routes and itineraries that guide visitors through the region's vineyards, châteaux, and picturesque landscapes. The "Route des Châteaux" in the Médoc region, for instance, takes you through the prestigious wine estates, allowing you to sample their wines and admire the architectural splendor of the châteaux. The "Saint-Émilion Wine Route" showcases the charming village of Saint-Émilion and its surrounding vineyards, providing a delightful exploration of the area's wine and cultural heritage.

Wine and Gastronomy:
Bordeaux is not only a paradise for wine lovers but also a culinary haven. The region's gastronomy perfectly complements its wines, with an abundance of Michelin-starred restaurants, charming bistros, and traditional eateries. Wine tourism in Bordeaux offers the opportunity to indulge in gourmet experiences, with food and wine pairings that showcase the local flavors and enhance the tasting experience. From farm-to-table delicacies to classic French cuisine, Bordeaux's culinary offerings are a treat for the senses.

In conclusion, wine tourism in Bordeaux provides an enriching and immersive experience for wine enthusiasts and travelers alike. From wine tastings and château visits to wine education programs and festive events, Bordeaux offers a wealth of opportunities to explore its world-class wines, vineyards, and cultural heritage. Whether you are a novice or an expert, a trip to Bordeaux will leave you with a profound appreciation for its wines and an unforgettable journey through one of the most prestigious wine regions in the world.

Wine Museums and Education Centers

Bordeaux, located in southwestern France, is renowned as one of the most prestigious and historic wine regions in the world. It is home to numerous vineyards, châteaux, and wineries, attracting wine enthusiasts from around the globe. In addition to its exquisite wines, Bordeaux offers a rich wine tourism experience through its wine museums and education centers, which provide visitors with an opportunity to delve into the region's winemaking heritage, learn about its diverse terroirs, and appreciate the art of wine production. Here, we explore some of the prominent wine museums and education centers in Bordeaux.

Cité du Vin: Located in the heart of Bordeaux, Cité du Vin is an iconic wine museum and cultural center dedicated to the world of wine. The building itself is an architectural masterpiece, resembling a swirling wine glass. Cité du Vin offers an immersive and interactive experience, showcasing the history, culture, and significance of wine through multimedia exhibitions, workshops, tastings, and events. Visitors can explore the museum's permanent collection, which includes artifacts, displays, and multimedia installations, or participate in guided tours and wine-themed workshops. The highlight of the visit is the Belvedere, an observation deck that provides panoramic views of Bordeaux while guests savor a glass of wine from around the world.

La Cité du Vin et du Négoce: Situated in the historic Chartrons district of Bordeaux, La Cité du Vin et du Négoce is a wine museum and educational center dedicated to the relationship between wine and trade. Housed in a renovated 18th-century building, this museum provides visitors with a unique insight into the commercial aspects of the wine industry. Through interactive exhibits, visitors can learn about the history of wine trade, the role of Bordeaux as a major trading hub, and the modern challenges faced by the industry. The museum also organizes tastings, workshops, and conferences, allowing visitors to deepen their knowledge and appreciation of Bordeaux wines.

Musée du Vin et du Négoce de Bordeaux:
Located in the heart of Bordeaux's historic district, the Musée du Vin et du Négoce de Bordeaux (Museum of Wine and Trade of Bordeaux) offers a comprehensive exploration of Bordeaux's wine heritage. Housed in a beautifully restored 18th-century cellar, the museum showcases the evolution of winemaking techniques, the history of wine trade, and the influence of Bordeaux wines on the world market. Visitors can explore the museum's vast collection of artifacts, including vintage bottles, cooperage tools, and ancient vineyard equipment. Guided tours and tastings are available, providing visitors with a deeper understanding of Bordeaux's viticultural traditions.

Maison du Vin de Bordeaux: Situated in the Chartrons district, the Maison du Vin de Bordeaux (House of Bordeaux Wine) is a wine education center dedicated to promoting Bordeaux wines and enhancing visitors' understanding of the region's terroir. The center offers various educational activities, including tastings, workshops, and seminars, led by knowledgeable wine professionals. Visitors can learn about different grape varieties, the classification system of Bordeaux wines, and the art of wine pairing. The Maison du Vin also serves as a platform for wine producers, providing a space for them to showcase their wines and interact with visitors.

These wine museums and education centers in Bordeaux offer a diverse range of experiences, catering to both casual wine enthusiasts and serious oenophiles. Whether you are interested in the history of winemaking, the commercial aspects of the wine industry, or simply wish to indulge in the beauty and flavors of Bordeaux wines, these institutions provide a wealth of knowledge, guided tastings, and cultural immersion. Exploring these wine museums and education centers is an enriching and unforgettable experience for anyone passionate about wine and its heritage.

Day Trips from Bordeaux

Arcachon

Arcachon, located on the southwestern coast of France, is a charming seaside town and a popular day trip destination from Bordeaux. Renowned for its stunning beaches, vibrant atmosphere, and natural beauty, Arcachon offers a delightful escape from the bustling city life of Bordeaux. This picturesque town is situated on the Arcachon Bay, known for its impressive sand dunes, oyster farming, and the iconic Dune du Pilat. With its diverse attractions and proximity to Bordeaux, Arcachon is a perfect choice for a day trip that combines relaxation, outdoor activities, and culinary delights.

Getting to Arcachon from Bordeaux is convenient and straightforward. The most convenient mode of transportation is by train, with regular services departing from Bordeaux Saint-Jean station. The journey takes approximately 50 minutes, offering scenic views of the countryside along the way. Alternatively, you can also opt for a car rental, which provides flexibility and allows you to explore the surrounding areas at your own pace.

Upon arrival in Arcachon, there are numerous activities and attractions to enjoy. The highlight of any visit to Arcachon is undoubtedly the Dune du Pilat, the tallest sand dune in Europe. Rising over 100 meters above sea level, this natural wonder offers breathtaking panoramic views of the bay, the Atlantic Ocean, and the surrounding pine forests. Climbing the dune can be a bit challenging but is well worth the effort. You can either walk up the sandy slope or use the stairs that have been installed for easier access.

Once at the top, take your time to admire the incredible scenery and capture memorable photographs.

Arcachon is also known for its beautiful beaches, which are perfect for sunbathing, swimming, and leisurely walks along the shore. Plage Pereire and Plage d'Eyrac are among the most popular beaches, offering golden sands and crystal-clear waters. If you're feeling adventurous, you can try water sports such as surfing, sailing, or paddleboarding, which are readily available along the coastline. Additionally, the calm waters of the Arcachon Bay are ideal for kayaking or taking a boat tour to explore the surrounding islands, including the famous Île aux Oiseaux (Bird Island).

Food enthusiasts will be delighted by the gastronomic offerings in Arcachon. The town is renowned for its fresh seafood, particularly its oysters, which are cultivated in the bay. You can indulge in a seafood feast at one of the many waterfront restaurants, where you can savor the flavors of local delicacies such as oysters, mussels, and prawns. The bustling city center is also home to a variety of charming cafes, bakeries, and ice cream parlors, offering delicious treats and refreshments.

For those interested in history and architecture, a visit to the Ville d'Hiver (Winter Town) is highly recommended. This elegant neighborhood showcases beautiful 19th-century villas and mansions, built during the town's heyday as a fashionable winter resort. Take a leisurely stroll through its tree-lined streets, admire the ornate Belle Époque architecture, and soak in the nostalgic atmosphere of a bygone era.

Finally, before leaving Arcachon, don't forget to explore the bustling town center and its vibrant markets. The Marché Municipal, located near the waterfront, is a must-visit destination for food lovers. Here you can find a wide array of fresh produce, seafood, cheeses, wines, and other regional specialties. The market offers an excellent opportunity to immerse yourself in the local culture and perhaps purchase some culinary souvenirs to take back home.

In conclusion, Arcachon offers a delightful day trip option from Bordeaux, combining natural beauty, seaside relaxation, and culinary delights. Whether you're climbing the majestic Dune du Pilat, enjoying the sandy beaches, indulging in fresh seafood, or exploring the charming town center, Arcachon has something to offer every traveler. Its close proximity to Bordeaux makes it an easily accessible destination, allowing visitors to experience the best of both worlds— the vibrant city life of Bordeaux and the tranquil coastal charm of Arcachon.

Dune du Pilat

Located on the southwestern coast of France, the Dune du Pilat (also known as the Dune of Pilat or the Great Dune of Pilat) is an iconic natural wonder and a popular day trip destination from Bordeaux. As the tallest sand dune in Europe, it offers breathtaking panoramic views of the Atlantic Ocean, the Arcachon Bay, and the surrounding pine forests. This majestic dune attracts thousands of visitors each year who come to witness its awe-inspiring beauty and indulge in outdoor activities.

Getting There:
The Dune du Pilat is situated approximately 60 kilometers southwest of Bordeaux, making it easily accessible for a day trip. The most convenient way to reach the dune is by car, which allows you to enjoy a scenic drive along the coastline. The journey takes around one hour, and there are parking facilities available near the dune. Additionally, you can opt for public transportation options such as trains and buses that operate between Bordeaux and Arcachon, the nearby town. From Arcachon, you can take a local bus or a taxi to reach the dune.

Exploring the Dune:
Upon arrival at the Dune du Pilat, you'll be greeted by an impressive sight—a vast expanse of sand stretching for approximately 2.7 kilometers in length, 500 meters in width, and towering up to 110 meters in height. As you

start ascending the dune, be prepared for a strenuous climb, as the sand can be soft and challenging to navigate. However, the effort is well worth it.

Reaching the top of the dune rewards you with breathtaking views that showcase the meeting point of land, sea, and sky. The azure waters of the Atlantic Ocean extend as far as the eye can see, and the neighboring Arcachon Bay glistens in the sunlight. On clear days, it's even possible to catch a glimpse of the distant Pyrenees mountains. The panoramic vista from the summit is truly awe-inspiring and provides a unique perspective on the natural beauty of the region.

Outdoor Activities:
Besides enjoying the spectacular views, the Dune du Pilat offers various outdoor activities for visitors to engage in. Many people choose to go sandboarding or sand-surfing down the slopes of the dune, creating an exhilarating experience as they glide through the fine grains of sand. The dune's gentle gradient makes it accessible for people of all ages and fitness levels to partake in these activities.

Alternatively, you can take leisurely walks along the dune's crest, breathing in the fresh sea air and taking in the scenic surroundings. The area is also perfect for a picnic, so consider bringing along some local delicacies and enjoy a relaxing lunch amidst the natural splendor.

Arcachon Bay:
While visiting the Dune du Pilat, you can also explore the neighboring Arcachon Bay. This stunning body of water is renowned for its oyster farming, and you can sample some of the freshest oysters in the local restaurants and markets. Take a boat trip to explore the bay, visit the charming town of Arcachon itself, or relax on one of the beautiful sandy beaches.

Practical Tips:

Dress appropriately for the climb, wearing comfortable shoes and sun protection as the sand can become hot under the sun.
It's advisable to bring water and snacks as there are limited facilities on the dune.
Consider visiting during weekdays or offseason periods to avoid crowds.
Remember to take your camera or smartphone to capture the stunning views from the top.

In conclusion, a day trip from Bordeaux to the Dune du Pilat is a remarkable experience that combines natural beauty, adventure, and relaxation. Whether you choose to climb to the summit, try sandboarding, or simply soak in the awe-inspiring scenery, this remarkable natural wonder will leave you with lasting memories of your visit to the Bordeaux region.

Saint-Émilion

Located in the heart of the renowned Bordeaux wine region, Saint-Émilion is a charming medieval village that offers an idyllic day trip destination from Bordeaux. With its historic architecture, picturesque vineyards, and exceptional wine heritage, Saint-Émilion attracts visitors from around the world who come to indulge in its rich cultural and gastronomic experiences. Here is a detailed guide to help you plan your day trip to Saint-Émilion.

Getting There:
Saint-Émilion is conveniently situated just 40 kilometers (25 miles) northeast of Bordeaux, making it easily accessible for a day trip. The most common way to reach Saint-Émilion from Bordeaux is by train. Trains run regularly from Bordeaux's main train station, Gare Saint-Jean, to Saint-Émilion. The journey takes approximately 30 minutes, and trains are comfortable and reliable.

Alternatively, you can also drive to Saint-Émilion, which provides the flexibility to explore the surrounding areas at your own pace. The journey takes around 45 minutes to an hour, depending on traffic conditions. Rental cars are available in Bordeaux if you don't have your own vehicle.

Exploring the Village:
Upon arriving in Saint-Émilion, you'll be greeted by a captivating village that exudes

medieval charm. The village is a UNESCO World Heritage site and is known for its narrow cobblestone streets, ancient stone buildings, and enchanting architecture.

Begin your exploration at the Place des Creneaux, a central square lined with inviting cafes and restaurants. From there, wander through the village's winding streets, admiring the well-preserved medieval structures and fascinating historical sites. Don't miss the Eglise Monolithe, a stunning monolithic church carved into the limestone rock. Inside, you'll find a remarkable underground network of catacombs and chapels.

Wine Tasting and Vineyard Visits:
Saint-Émilion is synonymous with exceptional wine, and a visit to this region wouldn't be complete without indulging in some wine tasting experiences. The village is surrounded by vineyards that produce some of the world's most prestigious wines.

Many wineries in Saint-Émilion welcome visitors for tours and tastings. You can choose to visit renowned châteaux like Château Ausone, Château Cheval Blanc, or Château Angélus, where you can learn about the winemaking process, explore the cellars, and sample a variety of wines.

If you prefer a more immersive experience, consider joining a guided tour that takes you to multiple wineries in the area. These tours often provide insight into the history and terroir of the region and are a great way to discover hidden gems.

Culinary Delights:
In addition to its wines, Saint-Émilion is also celebrated for its gastronomic offerings. The village is home to several gourmet restaurants and charming bistros where you can savor the flavors of the region.

Indulge in traditional French cuisine accompanied by a glass of Saint-Émilion wine, and sample local specialties such as cannelés (small caramelized pastries) and macarons. The charming ambiance of the village adds to the dining experience, making it a memorable part of your day trip.

Outdoor Activities:
If you're looking to explore the natural beauty surrounding Saint-Émilion, there are plenty of outdoor activities to enjoy. Take a leisurely

walk or rent a bicycle to venture into the rolling vineyards and enjoy the breathtaking landscapes.

The region is dotted with hiking trails that offer stunning views of the vine-covered hills. You can also embark on a boat trip along the Dordogne River, which runs nearby, to admire the picturesque scenery and vineyard-dotted landscapes from a different perspective.

Festivals and Events:
Throughout the year, Saint-Émilion hosts various festivals and events that showcase the region's rich cultural heritage. The most notable is the Jurade Festival, held on the third Sunday of June, which celebrates the local wine traditions with parades, tastings, and ceremonies.

During the harvest season, many wineries offer special events and grape-picking experiences, allowing visitors to actively participate in the winemaking process.

Conclusion:
A day trip from Bordeaux to Saint-Émilion is a delightful journey into the heart of French wine country. With its captivating medieval village,

world-class wines, and stunning landscapes, Saint-Émilion offers a perfect blend of history, culture, and gastronomy. Whether you're a wine enthusiast, a history buff, or simply seeking a peaceful retreat, Saint-Émilion is sure to leave a lasting impression and create cherished memories of your visit.

Cognac

If you find yourself in Bordeaux, France, and are looking for an exciting day trip, Cognac is an excellent choice. Located approximately 120 kilometers north of Bordeaux, Cognac is a charming town famous for its namesake brandy and picturesque vineyards. Here is a well-written and detailed guide to help you plan your day trip to Cognac.

Getting There:

To reach Cognac from Bordeaux, you have several transportation options. The most convenient way is to take a train from Bordeaux-Saint-Jean station to Cognac station. The journey takes around one hour, and the train provides a comfortable and scenic ride through the countryside. If you prefer driving, you can rent a car in Bordeaux and reach Cognac via the A10 highway. The drive takes approximately 1.5 hours, and it allows you to explore the beautiful landscapes of southwestern France.

Exploring the Town:

Once you arrive in Cognac, you'll be greeted by a charming town with a rich heritage. The town center is compact and easily navigable on foot. Start your exploration at the Place François 1er, a picturesque square lined with elegant 19th-century buildings. Here, you'll find the Tourist Office, where you can gather information about the town and its attractions.

Cognac Houses:

Cognac is renowned for its production of brandy, and a visit to one of the prestigious Cognac houses is a must. The most famous ones, such as Hennessy, Martell, Remy Martin, and Courvoisier, offer guided tours that take you through the fascinating process of creating Cognac. You'll learn about the distillation, aging, and blending techniques that contribute to the unique flavors of this renowned spirit. The tours often include tastings, allowing you to savor different Cognac varieties and gain a deeper appreciation for the craftsmanship behind them.

Cognac Museum:
To further delve into the history and culture of Cognac, a visit to the Cognac Museum is highly recommended. Housed in an impressive 15th-century former castle, the museum showcases the town's centuries-old relationship with the spirit. You'll discover the evolution of Cognac production, explore the traditional tools and equipment used in the past, and gain insights into the local traditions associated with this iconic beverage.

Boat Trips on the Charente River:
To experience Cognac from a different perspective, take a boat trip on the Charente River. Several operators offer scenic cruises that allow you to admire the vineyards, chateaux, and picturesque villages along the riverbanks. These cruises provide a relaxing

and enjoyable way to take in the natural beauty of the region and learn about the local history and heritage.

Lunch and Local Cuisine:
No trip to Cognac is complete without indulging in the delicious local cuisine. The town is home to several excellent restaurants where you can sample regional specialties. Don't miss the opportunity to savor dishes prepared with locally sourced ingredients, such as fresh seafood, Charentais melons, and the famous buttery Charentes-Poitou cheese. Pair your meal with a glass of Cognac or a local wine for an authentic culinary experience.

Nearby Vineyards:
If you have more time to spare, consider exploring the vineyards surrounding Cognac. The region boasts beautiful landscapes dotted with vineyards stretching as far as the eye can see. Many vineyards offer tours and tastings, allowing you to discover the nuances of the local grape varieties and the production of Cognac's essential ingredient, white wine. Visiting vineyards like Château de Beaulon or Domaine Rémy Martin provides a deeper understanding of the terroir and the

winemaking techniques that contribute to the region's renowned spirits.

Conclusion:

A day trip to Cognac from Bordeaux offers a delightful blend of history, culture, and gastronomy. From exploring the town's rich heritage to delving into the world of Cognac production, there are plenty of captivating experiences to enjoy. Whether you choose to visit the Cognac houses, the museum, take a boat trip, or venture into the vineyards, you'll come away with a deeper appreciation for this iconic French spirit and the picturesque region that produces it.

Médoc Wine Route

The Médoc region, located in southwestern France, is renowned for its prestigious vineyards and world-class wines. Just a short drive from Bordeaux, the capital of the Nouvelle-Aquitaine region, the Médoc Wine Route offers an excellent day trip for wine enthusiasts and those looking to explore the picturesque countryside. This well-traveled route takes visitors through charming villages, beautiful châteaux, and vineyards that produce some of the most esteemed wines in the world.

Getting There:
To embark on the Médoc Wine Route, start your journey from Bordeaux. The easiest way to reach the region is by car, as it provides the freedom to explore at your own pace. The total

driving distance is around 60 kilometers (37 miles) from Bordeaux, and the journey takes approximately one hour. Alternatively, you can also opt for guided tours or public transportation, such as buses or trains, which provide convenient options for those without a car.

Route Overview:
The Médoc Wine Route, officially known as "La Route des Châteaux," winds its way through the Médoc peninsula, which is bordered by the Atlantic Ocean to the west and the Gironde estuary to the east. The route stretches approximately 80 kilometers (50 miles) from north to south, passing through the renowned appellations of Margaux, Pauillac, Saint-Julien, and Saint-Estèphe, among others.

Châteaux and Vineyards:
The Médoc region is home to numerous prestigious châteaux and vineyards that have gained international recognition for their exceptional wines. Along the Médoc Wine Route, you'll have the opportunity to visit and tour some of these renowned estates, many of which are open to the public for tastings and visits.

Château Margaux, located in the appellation of Margaux, is one of the most prestigious wine estates in the Médoc. It boasts a rich history dating back to the 12th century and produces some of the finest wines in the world. The château offers guided tours of its cellars and vineyards, providing insights into the winemaking process and a chance to taste their exceptional wines.

Château Lafite Rothschild, situated in Pauillac, is another iconic estate worth visiting. With a history dating back to the 17th century, it has a reputation for producing wines of great elegance and longevity. While tours of the estate are by appointment only, the opportunity to witness the grandeur of the château and sample their exceptional wines makes for an unforgettable experience.

Château Lynch-Bages, also located in Pauillac, is a renowned estate with a history dating back to the 18th century. Known for its powerful and complex wines, Lynch-Bages offers guided tours of its vineyards, cellars, and a chance to taste their impressive selection of wines.

Village Explorations:

In addition to the châteaux and vineyards, the Médoc Wine Route takes you through charming villages that exude a rustic charm and provide glimpses into the region's history and culture.

Pauillac, the largest village on the Médoc peninsula, is an ideal place to start your exploration. Its picturesque waterfront promenade, lined with cafés and restaurants, offers stunning views of the Gironde estuary. Pauillac is also home to the Maison du Tourisme et du Vin, a visitor center where you can learn more about the region's wines and plan your itinerary.

The village of Saint-Julien, nestled between Margaux and Pauillac, is known for its elegant wines. Here, you can wander through its narrow streets, admire its charming architecture, and perhaps even visit one of the smaller châteaux in the area.

Soussans, a small village located in the heart of the Margaux appellation, offers a peaceful respite from the bustling wine estates. Explore its quaint streets, visit the local church, and soak in the tranquil ambiance of this charming village.

Gastronomy and Cuisine:
A visit to the Médoc region is not complete without indulging in its exceptional gastronomy. Many of the châteaux and villages along the Médoc Wine Route offer opportunities to savor the local cuisine and pair it with the region's wines.

Numerous restaurants and bistros in the area showcase the richness of Médoc's culinary traditions, offering delicious dishes prepared with locally sourced ingredients. From traditional French cuisine to seafood specialties, there is something to please every palate.

Conclusion:
A day trip along the Médoc Wine Route from Bordeaux is an immersive experience that combines stunning landscapes, prestigious vineyards, and exceptional wines. Whether you're a wine enthusiast or simply appreciate the beauty of the French countryside, exploring this renowned wine region will leave you with lasting memories and a deeper appreciation for the art of winemaking.

Gastronomy in Bordeaux

Bordeaux Culinary Delights

Bordeaux, the world-renowned wine capital of France, is not only famous for its exceptional vineyards but also for its culinary delights. The region's gastronomy is deeply rooted in its rich history, culture, and the bountiful produce that surrounds it. From exquisite seafood to succulent meats, and a plethora of delightful pastries, Bordeaux offers a diverse range of flavors that tantalize the taste buds of locals and visitors alike. In this article, we will explore the culinary delights of Bordeaux and delve into the essence of its gastronomic scene.

Seafood plays a prominent role in Bordeaux's culinary offerings. The region's proximity to the Atlantic Ocean ensures a steady supply of fresh fish and shellfish. Oysters, in particular, are a local specialty and are best enjoyed with a glass of crisp white wine from the nearby vineyards. Bordeaux's oyster farmers have mastered the art of cultivating these delicacies, and you can savor their briny goodness in various forms, including raw, grilled, or incorporated into mouthwatering seafood platters.

Moving beyond seafood, Bordeaux is also renowned for its exceptional meats. The region is home to some of the finest beef in the world, most notably the famed Blonde d'Aquitaine breed. The local cattle are raised in lush pastures, resulting in tender and flavorful meat. A classic dish that showcases Bordeaux's beef is the entrecôte à la bordelaise, a juicy rib-eye steak served with a rich red wine sauce. The marriage of Bordeaux wine and beef is a match made in culinary heaven.

Speaking of wine, it would be remiss not to mention the integral role it plays in Bordeaux's gastronomy. The region boasts over 6,000 vineyards, producing some of the world's finest wines. From the prestigious classified growths of the Médoc to the sweet nectars of Sauternes, Bordeaux offers a diverse range of wines to accompany its culinary delights. Wine tasting and food pairing experiences are a must for visitors, where you can sample the exquisite flavors of Bordeaux's reds, whites, and dessert wines while indulging in local delicacies.

No culinary journey in Bordeaux would be complete without exploring its vibrant farmers' markets. These bustling hubs of gastronomic delight are filled with an array of fresh produce, artisanal cheeses, bread, and pastries. The Marché des Capucins, located in the heart of Bordeaux, is a food lover's paradise. Here, you can discover seasonal fruits, aromatic herbs, regional cheeses like the creamy Époisses, and indulge in the famous canelé—a small, caramelized pastry with a soft custard center.

When it comes to desserts, Bordeaux has its fair share of sweet temptations. One iconic treat is the canelé, previously mentioned, which originated in the city. These small, caramelized cakes with a custardy interior are a delightful way to end a meal. Another beloved dessert is the dacquoise, a layered confection made with almond meringue and filled with various flavors such as chocolate, coffee, or fruit. Paired with a sweet white wine, these desserts are the perfect finale to a memorable meal.

In summary, Bordeaux's gastronomy is a celebration of the region's natural abundance, centuries-old traditions, and impeccable craftsmanship. From the freshest seafood to succulent meats, delectable pastries, and world-class wines, the culinary delights of Bordeaux are sure to leave a lasting impression on any food lover. Whether you explore the vibrant markets, dine in Michelin-starred restaurants, or simply savor the local flavors at a cozy bistro, Bordeaux's culinary scene is a feast for the senses, inviting you to embark on an unforgettable gastronomic adventure.

Best Restaurants in Bordeaux

Bordeaux, located in the southwestern part of France, is renowned for its exquisite wines. However, the city's culinary scene is equally impressive, making it a top destination for food lovers. Bordeaux boasts a rich gastronomic heritage, blending traditional French cuisine with innovative techniques and local produce. In this guide, we will explore some of the best restaurants in Bordeaux, offering a diverse range of dining experiences to suit every palate.

La Tupina:
Tucked away in the heart of the historic district, La Tupina is a true gem of Bordeaux's culinary scene. This rustic restaurant captures the essence of traditional Gascon cuisine, with a focus on hearty, comforting dishes. The menu features specialties like confit duck, foie gras,

and slow-cooked stews. The charming ambiance and warm hospitality make La Tupina a must-visit for those seeking an authentic taste of Bordeaux.

Le Chapon Fin:
Housed in a beautifully restored 18th-century building, Le Chapon Fin is a Michelin-starred restaurant that showcases the elegance of French fine dining. Led by talented chef Nicolas Frion, the menu highlights seasonal ingredients and offers a harmonious blend of flavors and textures. The culinary creations at Le Chapon Fin are not only visually stunning but also delight the taste buds with their meticulous attention to detail.

Garopapilles:
For a unique dining experience, Garopapilles combines art, wine, and gastronomy. This Michelin-starred restaurant, located in the Chartrons neighborhood, is known for its exceptional wine selection and innovative cuisine. The chef, Tanguy Laviale, creates a seasonal menu that showcases local produce and incorporates unexpected flavor combinations. The contemporary decor and knowledgeable sommeliers add to the overall charm of the place.

Miles:
Situated in the Saint-Pierre district, Miles is a modern and stylish restaurant that offers a refreshing take on traditional French cuisine. The menu is inspired by global flavors and incorporates a variety of textures and techniques. Expect dishes like roasted cod with miso, crispy pork belly with ginger, and creative desserts. With its vibrant atmosphere and culinary creativity, Miles attracts both locals and tourists alike.

Le Petit Commerce:
If you're in the mood for seafood, Le Petit Commerce is the place to go. This beloved institution has been serving the finest seafood in Bordeaux since 1901. The menu features fresh oysters, mussels, shrimp, and an array of fish cooked to perfection. The rustic decor and convivial atmosphere make it a favorite among locals who appreciate high-quality seafood in a casual setting.

L'Entrecôte:
For a classic French steak experience, L'Entrecôte is a popular choice. Located near the Place des Quinconces, this restaurant specializes in serving prime cuts of beef

accompanied by their secret sauce and crispy fries. The simplicity of the menu allows the focus to be on the quality of the meat, ensuring a memorable dining experience for steak enthusiasts.

Le Pressoir d'Argent:
If you're looking for a fine dining experience with a touch of luxury, Le Pressoir d'Argent is the epitome of elegance. Situated within the prestigious InterContinental Bordeaux - Le Grand Hotel, this two-Michelin-starred restaurant is helmed by renowned chef Gordon Ramsay. The menu showcases innovative and refined dishes, highlighting the best ingredients from the region. Impeccable service and a stunning dining room contribute to an unforgettable gastronomic journey.

These are just a few of the exceptional restaurants Bordeaux has to offer. From traditional French cuisine to cutting-edge gastronomy, the city's dining scene caters to a range of tastes and budgets. Whether you're a wine enthusiast or a food lover, exploring the culinary delights of Bordeaux is sure to be a memorable experience.

Markets and Food Experiences

Bordeaux, the vibrant and historic city nestled in the heart of France's renowned wine region, is not only famous for its vineyards but also for its exceptional gastronomy. With a rich culinary heritage, Bordeaux offers a diverse range of markets and food experiences that cater to both locals and visitors alike. In this article, we will explore the highlights of Bordeaux's gastronomy scene, including its markets and the unique food experiences they offer.

Markets in Bordeaux:

Bordeaux is home to several bustling markets where you can find an array of fresh produce, local specialties, and artisanal products. Here are some of the most popular markets in the city:

a. Marché des Capucins: Located in the heart of Bordeaux, Marché des Capucins is one of the oldest and largest markets in the city. This vibrant covered market is a food lover's paradise, offering a wide range of fresh fruits, vegetables, seafood, cheese, charcuterie, spices, and more. The market is also home to various food stalls and small eateries where you can indulge in regional delicacies such as oysters, duck confit, and canelés, a traditional Bordeaux pastry.

b. Marché des Quais: Situated along the Garonne River, Marché des Quais is a picturesque market that takes place every Sunday. It showcases a variety of local and organic products, including fruits, vegetables, bread, cheese, wine, and honey. The market has a relaxed atmosphere, and you can enjoy a leisurely stroll while savoring samples of the region's finest offerings.

c. Marché des Grands Hommes: Located in the elegant Triangle d'Or district, Marché des Grands Hommes is a high-end market known for its upscale products. Here, you will find gourmet foods, premium meats, seafood, truffles, caviar, and an impressive selection of wines. The market also houses specialty shops where you can purchase culinary treasures to take home as souvenirs.

Food Experiences:
Apart from the markets, Bordeaux offers a range of food experiences that allow visitors to immerse themselves in the city's gastronomic

culture. Here are a few noteworthy experiences:

a. Wine Tours and Tastings: Given Bordeaux's status as one of the world's most esteemed wine regions, no visit would be complete without exploring its vineyards and enjoying wine tastings. Numerous tour operators offer guided tours to vineyards in the nearby Médoc, Saint-Émilion, and Pessac-Léognan appellations, where you can learn about the winemaking process and sample a variety of wines, including the region's iconic red blends.

b. Cooking Classes: Enhance your culinary skills by participating in a cooking class led by experienced chefs in Bordeaux. These classes provide hands-on experiences where you can learn to prepare classic Bordeaux dishes, such as boeuf bordelaise (beef stewed in red wine), confit de canard (duck confit), and tarte aux fraises (strawberry tart). You'll get insights into local ingredients, cooking techniques, and the art of food pairing.

c. Michelin-Starred Dining: Bordeaux boasts several Michelin-starred restaurants, offering unforgettable gastronomic experiences. These establishments showcase the region's finest ingredients and the culinary mastery of renowned chefs. From innovative contemporary cuisine to traditional dishes reinvented with a modern twist, the city's Michelin-starred restaurants cater to discerning palates and guarantee an exceptional dining experience.

In conclusion, Bordeaux's gastronomy scene is a treasure trove for food enthusiasts. The city's markets provide a vibrant and authentic experience, allowing you to sample the freshest produce and regional specialties. Additionally, the diverse food experiences available, such as wine tours, cooking classes, and Michelin-starred dining, offer unique opportunities to delve deeper into Bordeaux's culinary heritage. Whether you're a food lover, wine connoisseur, or simply someone who appreciates the art of gastronomy, Bordeaux is sure to leave you with a memorable and satisfying culinary journey.

Outdoor Activities in Bordeaux

Cycling and Bike Paths

Bordeaux, the vibrant city in southwestern France renowned for its rich history, stunning architecture, and world-class wine, offers a plethora of outdoor activities for visitors and locals alike. Among the most popular activities is cycling, thanks to the city's extensive network of bike paths and its commitment to creating a bicycle-friendly environment. Whether you're a leisure cyclist or an avid enthusiast, Bordeaux provides numerous opportunities to explore its charming streets, picturesque countryside, and scenic riverbanks.

Bike Paths in Bordeaux:
Bordeaux boasts an impressive network of bike paths, making it easy and safe to navigate the city and its surrounding areas on two wheels. The city's commitment to cycling infrastructure has resulted in over 580 kilometers (360 miles) of bike paths, ensuring cyclists can traverse Bordeaux and its neighboring towns without having to contend with heavy traffic. These

bike paths are well-marked, clearly designated, and separate from motorized vehicles, ensuring a pleasant and secure cycling experience.

La Piste Cyclable Roger Lapébie:
One of the most popular and picturesque bike paths in Bordeaux is the Roger Lapébie cycle path, named after the French cyclist Roger Lapébie, who won the Tour de France in 1937. This scenic trail stretches over 58 kilometers (36 miles) and follows an old railway line, offering a delightful route through vineyards, forests, and charming villages. The path starts in Bordeaux and takes cyclists through the heart of the Entre-Deux-Mers wine region, passing through Creon, Sauveterre-de-Guyenne, and continuing all the way to Sauveterre-de-Guyenne.

La Voie Verte de Bordeaux-Lac:
The Voie Verte de Bordeaux-Lac is another popular cycling route, offering a beautiful and easily accessible path for cyclists of all levels. This 14-kilometer (8.7-mile) path starts near the Bordeaux-Lac Exhibition Center and follows the eastern shore of Lake Bordeaux, providing stunning views of the water and surrounding greenery. The trail continues through lush parks, gardens, and picnic areas,

making it an excellent choice for a leisurely ride or a family outing.

Quais de Bordeaux:
For those looking to explore the heart of Bordeaux, the Quais de Bordeaux provides a scenic route along the Garonne River. This path stretches for approximately 5 kilometers (3.1 miles) and offers breathtaking views of the city's iconic waterfront, historic buildings, and bustling riverbanks. The wide and well-maintained path is shared by cyclists, pedestrians, and rollerbladers, creating a lively atmosphere. Cyclists can enjoy the beautiful surroundings and access various attractions, such as the Place de la Bourse, Pont de Pierre, and the charming Chartrons neighborhood.

Bordeaux to Saint-Émilion:
Cycling enthusiasts and wine lovers will delight in the bike path that connects Bordeaux to the picturesque village of Saint-Émilion. This 35-kilometer (22-mile) route takes cyclists through the heart of the renowned Bordeaux wine region, passing vineyards, châteaux, and idyllic countryside landscapes. The path is relatively flat, allowing riders to fully appreciate the beauty of the region without encountering challenging terrain. Upon

reaching Saint-Émilion, cyclists can explore the medieval village, visit world-class wineries, and indulge in the local gastronomy.

Bicycle Rental and Services:
Bordeaux offers various options for renting bicycles, catering to different preferences and needs. There are numerous bike rental shops throughout the city, particularly near popular tourist areas and train stations. Several companies offer both traditional bicycles and electric bikes (e-bikes) for rent, allowing cyclists to effortlessly explore Bordeaux and its surroundings. Additionally, many hotels and accommodations provide bicycle rentals as a convenient service for their guests.

Bordeaux also features an extensive bike-sharing system known as VCub, which provides self-service bicycles for short-term rentals. With over 1,800 bikes and 179 stations located throughout the city, VCub offers a convenient and eco-friendly means of transportation for visitors and residents alike. Users can easily rent and return bicycles at any VCub station using a credit card or an annual subscription.

Safety and Regulations:

When cycling in Bordeaux, it's important to adhere to safety regulations and practice responsible biking. Wearing a helmet is highly recommended, especially for longer rides or when venturing into busy traffic areas. Cyclists should also familiarize themselves with the local traffic laws and respect the rights of pedestrians and other cyclists. It's essential to use hand signals, stay on designated bike paths whenever possible, and exercise caution when sharing the road with vehicles.

In conclusion, Bordeaux offers an exceptional range of outdoor activities, with cycling being a fantastic way to explore the city and its surrounding areas. The extensive network of bike paths, including the Roger Lapébie cycle path, the Voie Verte de Bordeaux-Lac, the Quais de Bordeaux, and the Bordeaux to Saint-Émilion route, provides cyclists with diverse and picturesque routes to suit all preferences and abilities. With the availability of bike rentals and the city's commitment to cycling infrastructure, Bordeaux truly stands out as a premier destination for outdoor enthusiasts and bike lovers alike.

Water Sports on the Garonne River

Bordeaux, a vibrant city in southwestern France, offers a wide array of outdoor activities for adventure enthusiasts. Nestled along the picturesque Garonne River, the city provides a perfect playground for water sports enthusiasts. Whether you're an adrenaline junkie or simply seeking a fun-filled day on the water, Bordeaux has something to offer everyone. In this guide, we will explore the exciting world of water sports on the Garonne River.

Kayaking and Canoeing:
Kayaking and canoeing are popular water sports activities on the Garonne River. With its calm waters and stunning backdrop, the river provides an excellent setting for paddling adventures. Several kayak and canoe rental companies offer equipment and guided tours to suit all skill levels. Whether you're a beginner or an experienced paddler, you can explore the river at your own pace, taking in the beautiful sights of Bordeaux's waterfront and historic landmarks.

Stand-Up Paddleboarding (SUP):
Stand-up paddleboarding has gained popularity in recent years, and Bordeaux's

Garonne River is an ideal spot to enjoy this activity. SUP allows you to stand on a large surfboard-like paddleboard and use a long paddle to navigate the water. It's a fantastic way to explore the river and engage your core muscles while enjoying the scenic views of Bordeaux's skyline. SUP rentals and lessons are readily available, making it accessible to both beginners and experienced paddlers.

Wakeboarding and Waterskiing:
For those seeking a more exhilarating water sports experience, wakeboarding and waterskiing are excellent choices on the Garonne River. These activities involve being towed behind a speedboat while standing on a wakeboard or skis. Wakeboarding combines elements of snowboarding, surfing, and skateboarding, providing an adrenaline rush as you glide across the water and perform tricks. Waterskiing involves skiing on two skis or a single ski while being towed by a boat. Numerous wakeboard and waterski schools cater to all levels of expertise, from beginners to advanced riders, providing lessons and equipment rentals.

River Cruises:

If you prefer a more relaxed water-based activity, consider taking a river cruise on the Garonne River. Various companies offer sightseeing tours and dinner cruises, allowing you to enjoy the tranquil beauty of Bordeaux from the water. These cruises often include informative commentary about the city's history and landmarks, making it a delightful way to explore Bordeaux while enjoying a leisurely ride on the river.

Jet Skiing:
Jet skiing is a thrilling water sport that lets you speed across the Garonne River, creating waves of excitement. You can rent jet skis and explore the river's stretches, feeling the rush of adrenaline as you navigate the water on these powerful machines. Jet skiing is a great option for adventure seekers who crave speed and excitement.

Safety Considerations:
While engaging in water sports activities on the Garonne River, it is essential to prioritize safety. Follow all safety guidelines provided by rental companies, wear appropriate safety equipment such as life jackets, and be aware of your surroundings. It's also advisable to check weather conditions before heading out on the

water and avoid strong currents or unfavorable weather.

In conclusion, Bordeaux's Garonne River offers a fantastic playground for water sports enthusiasts. From kayaking and stand-up paddleboarding to wakeboarding and jet skiing, there are activities to suit every taste and skill level. Whether you're seeking adventure or relaxation, exploring the river's waters will provide unforgettable experiences and stunning views of Bordeaux's captivating landscape. So, grab your gear, embrace the thrill, and dive into the exciting world of water sports in Bordeaux.

Golfing in Bordeaux

Bordeaux, located in southwestern France, is renowned for its stunning vineyards, historical architecture, and rich cultural heritage. While wine tourism is a popular activity in the region, Bordeaux also offers a range of outdoor activities, including golfing. With its mild climate, picturesque landscapes, and top-notch golf courses, Bordeaux provides a fantastic destination for golf enthusiasts of all skill levels. Here is a detailed guide to golfing in Bordeaux.

Golf Courses:
Bordeaux boasts several exceptional golf courses that cater to different preferences and skill levels. Here are a few notable ones:

a. Golf du Médoc Resort: This renowned golf complex is located in the heart of the Médoc vineyards, just a 20-minute drive from Bordeaux city center. It offers two 18-hole championship courses, the Châteaux Course and the Vignes Course. The Châteaux Course, designed by Bill Coore, presents a traditional Scottish links-style layout, while the Vignes Course, designed by Rodney Wright and John Harris, features more water hazards and undulating fairways.

b. Golf de Bordeaux-Cameyrac: Situated in the peaceful surroundings of the Entre-Deux-Mers region, this 18-hole course is known for its stunning scenery and varied challenges. Designed by Tom Doak, the course incorporates the natural landscape, with trees, lakes, and streams adding to the visual appeal. The layout is suitable for players of all levels, offering a fair yet demanding experience.

c. Golf Blue Green Bordeaux-Lac: Located near Lake Bordeaux and easily accessible from the city center, this 36-hole golf complex is ideal for golfers seeking convenience. The facility consists of two 18-hole courses, the Red Course and the Yellow Course, both offering a mix of parkland and woodland settings. The Red Course is more technical, with narrow fairways and water hazards, while the Yellow Course is more forgiving and suitable for beginners.

Golf Facilities and Amenities:
Most golf courses in Bordeaux offer excellent facilities and amenities to enhance your golfing experience. These typically include:

a. Clubhouse: Each golf course has a clubhouse where you can relax, socialize, and enjoy a meal or refreshments. Clubhouses often offer panoramic views of the course and provide comfortable spaces to unwind after your round.

b. Practice Areas: Golf courses usually feature practice facilities such as driving ranges, putting greens, and chipping areas. These areas allow you to warm up before your round or improve your skills through focused practice.

c. Golf Lessons: If you're new to golf or looking to refine your technique, many courses in Bordeaux offer golf lessons with experienced instructors. These lessons can be tailored to your skill level and provide valuable insights to help you improve your game.

d. Pro Shops: Golf courses often have pro shops where you can purchase or rent golf equipment, clothing, and accessories. These shops stock a wide range of products from leading brands, ensuring you have everything you need for your golfing experience.

Additional Tips:

a. Booking: It is advisable to book your tee times in advance, especially during peak seasons or weekends, to secure your preferred playing slot.

b. Equipment: If you prefer to travel light, you can rent golf clubs and other equipment from the golf courses. However, if you have your own set of clubs, it is recommended to bring them along for familiarity and comfort.

c. Dress Code: Most golf courses have a dress code, so it's essential to check their requirements before your visit. Generally, collared shirts, tailored trousers or shorts, and golf shoes are considered appropriate attire.

d. Transportation: While some golf courses are easily accessible by public transportation or taxis, renting a car or using a ride-sharing service might be more convenient for reaching certain courses located outside the city center.

Golfing in Bordeaux offers a wonderful combination of challenging courses, breathtaking scenery, and the opportunity to immerse yourself in the region's natural beauty. Whether you're a seasoned golfer or a beginner looking to take up the sport, Bordeaux's golf courses provide a memorable experience for all. So pack your clubs, enjoy the lush fairways, and savor the exceptional golfing opportunities in this picturesque region of France.

Hiking and Nature Trails

Bordeaux, located in southwestern France, is renowned for its world-class vineyards and exquisite architecture. However, the region surrounding Bordeaux also offers a plethora of opportunities for outdoor enthusiasts seeking to explore nature and embark on hiking and nature trails. From picturesque vineyards to lush forests and stunning coastal landscapes, there is something for everyone to enjoy. In this guide, we will delve into some of the best outdoor activities in Bordeaux, focusing specifically on hiking and nature trails.

Medoc Natural Park:
Situated northwest of Bordeaux, the Medoc Natural Park boasts an enchanting landscape of sand dunes, marshes, forests, and coastline. With over 200 kilometers of marked trails, this park provides ample opportunities for hikers to discover its diverse flora and fauna. The trails meander through pine forests, offering shade and tranquility, while the coastal paths provide stunning views of the Atlantic Ocean. Keep an eye out for unique bird species, such as the European spoonbill and osprey, as you explore this pristine natural haven.

Les Landes de Gascogne Regional Nature Park:
Located south of Bordeaux, Les Landes de Gascogne Regional Nature Park is the largest forested area in Europe. Spanning over one

million hectares, this vast park offers a myriad of hiking trails suitable for all levels of expertise. From short leisurely walks to long-distance treks, visitors can immerse themselves in the peaceful ambiance of this magnificent forest. The park also features numerous lakes and rivers, providing opportunities for fishing, canoeing, and kayaking.

Entre-Deux-Mers:
Situated between the Garonne and Dordogne rivers, the Entre-Deux-Mers region is renowned for its rolling hills, charming villages, and vineyards. The area is crisscrossed by an extensive network of hiking trails, which allow visitors to explore the picturesque countryside and enjoy the scenic beauty of the region. Along the way, you can discover medieval castles, Romanesque churches, and sample delicious wines produced in the area. The Entre-Deux-Mers region offers a blend of cultural heritage and natural splendor, making it a must-visit destination for outdoor enthusiasts.

Dune du Pilat:
Just an hour's drive from Bordeaux, Dune du Pilat is the tallest sand dune in Europe and a natural wonder that shouldn't be missed.

Hiking to the summit of the dune rewards you with breathtaking panoramic views of the Atlantic Ocean, the Landes forest, and the Banc d'Arguin Nature Reserve. The climb can be physically demanding, but the experience is well worth the effort. You can also explore the surrounding pine forests and enjoy a stroll along the sandy beaches nearby.

The GR® de Pays Estuaire de la Gironde: For those seeking a longer hiking adventure, the GR® de Pays Estuaire de la Gironde is a fantastic option. This long-distance trail follows the meandering Gironde estuary, offering spectacular vistas and glimpses of historic landmarks along the way. The trail passes through picturesque villages, vineyards, and marshlands, allowing hikers to appreciate the beauty and diversity of the region. The entire trail stretches over 120 kilometers, but you can choose to explore shorter sections based on your preference and available time.

Before embarking on any hiking or nature trail in Bordeaux, it's essential to be well-prepared. Ensure you have suitable footwear, sufficient water, and snacks for the journey. Additionally, be mindful of weather conditions and follow any safety guidelines provided by the local authorities or park management.

With its diverse landscapes and natural wonders, Bordeaux offers an array of outdoor activities for hiking enthusiasts. Whether you prefer coastal walks, forest treks, or vineyard trails, there is a trail waiting to be explored in this captivating region. So, put on your hiking boots, pack your backpack, and set out to discover the enchanting outdoor beauty of Bordeaux.

Adventure Parks and Recreation

Bordeaux, located in the southwestern region of France, is renowned for its world-class wine, rich history, and stunning architecture. However, this vibrant city also offers a wide array of outdoor activities for adventure enthusiasts and nature lovers alike. From adventure parks to recreational options, Bordeaux has something to offer everyone seeking an adrenaline rush or a serene escape into nature. Let's explore some of the top outdoor activities in Bordeaux, including adventure parks and recreational options.

Darwin Ecosystem:
Situated on the right bank of the Garonne River, Darwin Ecosystem is a unique urban oasis and a hub for outdoor activities. This former military barracks turned eco-district offers a variety of adventure sports and recreational facilities. From skateboarding and BMX biking at one of Europe's largest outdoor skate parks to climbing at the indoor climbing gym, Darwin Ecosystem provides plenty of options for thrill-seekers. Additionally, you can try out paddleboarding or kayaking on the river, or simply relax and enjoy the vibrant atmosphere of this sustainable community.

Forest Adventure:
Located just a short drive from Bordeaux, Forest Adventure is an exciting treetop adventure park nestled in the heart of a beautiful forest. It offers a thrilling experience for visitors of all ages. With various circuits and levels of difficulty, you can test your agility and balance while navigating through zip lines, suspension bridges, and tree platforms. The park provides a safe environment and professional instructors who ensure your safety while delivering an unforgettable outdoor adventure.

Cap Sciences:

Cap Sciences, an interactive science museum located on the banks of the Garonne River, offers a range of outdoor activities that combine learning and fun. The museum features a rooftop terrace known as "Jardin des Étoiles" (Garden of Stars), where visitors can participate in astronomy workshops, stargazing sessions, and even observe the sun through telescopes. The terrace also provides a stunning panoramic view of Bordeaux. Cap Sciences frequently organizes outdoor events and exhibitions related to science, technology, and nature, making it an excellent choice for families and curious minds.

Parc Bordelais:

For those seeking a more relaxed outdoor experience, Parc Bordelais is an ideal destination. This expansive public park, spanning over 28 hectares, offers a peaceful retreat from the bustling city. The park features vast lawns, beautiful flower beds, and shady paths perfect for leisurely walks, picnics, or bike rides. You can rent a boat and navigate the serene lake, enjoy a game of tennis, or let your children have fun on the playgrounds. Parc

Bordelais is a beloved green space cherished by locals and visitors alike.

Lacanau-Océan:
If you're willing to venture a bit farther from Bordeaux, about 55 kilometers away, Lacanau-Océan awaits you. This coastal town offers an array of outdoor activities, particularly focused on water sports and beachside relaxation. Known for its excellent surfing conditions, Lacanau-Océan attracts surfers from around the world. Beginners can take lessons at one of the surf schools, while experienced surfers can catch waves at various spots along the coastline. Additionally, you can try kiteboarding, windsurfing, or simply unwind on the sandy beaches and soak up the sun.

Bordeaux's outdoor activities cater to both thrill-seekers and those seeking a tranquil escape into nature. Whether you prefer adrenaline-pumping adventures or leisurely pursuits, the city and its surroundings provide numerous options to make your outdoor experience unforgettable.

Shopping in Bordeaux

Shopping Districts

Bordeaux, the vibrant city in southwestern France renowned for its wine and rich history, offers an exceptional shopping experience. With its mix of traditional and modern elements, Bordeaux boasts several distinct shopping districts that cater to a variety of tastes and preferences. Whether you're searching for luxury brands, local specialties, or unique boutiques, Bordeaux has something for everyone. Here are some of the top shopping districts in Bordeaux:

Rue Sainte-Catherine:
Rue Sainte-Catherine is Bordeaux's main shopping street and one of the longest pedestrian shopping streets in Europe. Stretching over 1.2 kilometers, it runs from Place de la Comédie to Place de la Victoire. This bustling avenue is home to numerous international and national retail chains, high-street fashion brands, department stores, and popular franchises. You'll find well-known names like Zara, H&M, Galeries Lafayette, and Sephora, among others. Rue Sainte-Catherine

is perfect for fashion enthusiasts and those seeking a wide range of options under one roof.

Triangle d'Or:
Located in the heart of Bordeaux's historic center, the Triangle d'Or (Golden Triangle) is an upscale shopping district that exudes elegance and luxury. Bordered by Cours de l'Intendance, Allées de Tourny, and Cours Clemenceau, this area is known for its high-end boutiques, designer brands, and prestigious jewelry stores. Some of the renowned fashion houses found here include Louis Vuitton, Hermès, Chanel, and Gucci. In addition to fashion, the Triangle d'Or also offers art galleries, antique shops, and gourmet food stores, making it a sophisticated destination for discerning shoppers.

Quai des Marques:
Located on the right bank of the Garonne River, Quai des Marques is a trendy shopping district housed in refurbished warehouses. This open-air shopping village offers a mix of factory outlets, discount stores, and designer shops. Quai des Marques is known for its discounted prices on well-known brands such as Nike, Levis, The North Face, and Calvin Klein. It's a great place to find quality products

at affordable prices. Additionally, the location along the waterfront provides a scenic backdrop while you indulge in your shopping spree.

Chartrons:

The Chartrons neighborhood, located north of the city center, is a trendy and artistic district that attracts a diverse range of shoppers. Known for its antique shops, art galleries, and concept stores, Chartrons is a haven for those seeking unique and eclectic items. This district is particularly famous for its antique dealers and vintage shops, offering a wide array of furniture, decorative objects, and collectibles. Additionally, you'll find contemporary art galleries showcasing local and international artists, making Chartrons a must-visit for art enthusiasts and collectors.

Marché des Capucins:

If you're in search of a vibrant and authentic shopping experience, head to Marché des Capucins. This bustling covered market, situated near Place de la Victoire, is the largest daily market in Bordeaux. Here you'll find an impressive selection of fresh produce, local delicacies, cheese, seafood, and regional wines. The market is a feast for the senses, with colorful stalls, enticing aromas, and lively ambiance. It's the perfect place to immerse yourself in the local food culture and pick up some ingredients for a picnic or a culinary souvenir.

In conclusion, Bordeaux offers a diverse range of shopping districts, each with its own unique character and offerings. Whether you prefer high-street fashion, luxury brands, antiques, or fresh produce, Bordeaux has an array of choices to satisfy every shopper's desires. So, explore these districts and discover the charm and delights of shopping in Bordeaux.

Local Products and Souvenirs

Bordeaux, the capital city of the Nouvelle-Aquitaine region in southwestern France, is renowned for its rich history, stunning architecture, and, of course, its world-famous wines. In addition to its cultural and gastronomic delights, Bordeaux offers a fantastic shopping experience with a wide array of local products and souvenirs to choose from. Whether you're a wine aficionado, a fashion enthusiast, or someone seeking unique gifts, Bordeaux has something to offer for everyone. Let's delve into the delightful world of shopping in Bordeaux, exploring its local products and souvenirs.

Wine and Spirits:
Bordeaux is synonymous with exceptional wines, so it's no surprise that wine-related products dominate the local market. You'll find an extensive selection of Bordeaux wines, ranging from prestigious châteaux to affordable yet delightful bottles. Visit specialty wine shops such as L'Intendant or Maison du Vin de Bordeaux to explore the vast collection. You can also find wine-related accessories like corkscrews, decanters, and wine glasses, perfect for wine connoisseurs.

Gastronomic Delights:
In addition to wine, Bordeaux boasts a thriving food scene. Local delicacies like canelés (small, caramelized pastries), foie gras, truffles, and locally-produced chocolates are among the gastronomic delights you'll find in Bordeaux. Head to La Maison Darricau or Les Délices de Bordeaux to discover these delectable treats and take home a taste of Bordeaux's culinary heritage.

Fashion and Accessories:
Bordeaux offers a wide range of fashion boutiques, from high-end designer stores to trendy local shops. The city is known for its chic and sophisticated style, blending contemporary fashion with classic elegance. Rue Sainte-Catherine, one of the longest pedestrian shopping streets in Europe, is a shopaholic's paradise, housing international brands, local designers, and popular department stores. For unique accessories and jewelry, explore the charming boutiques in the Saint-Pierre neighborhood.

Antiques and Vintage:
If you're a fan of antiques and vintage treasures, Bordeaux has a plethora of shops and markets to satisfy your cravings. The Chartrons neighborhood, with its picturesque streets and antique dealers, is the perfect place to start. Here, you'll find a diverse range of antique furniture, vintage clothing, art, and collectibles. The Quai des Chartrons market, held on Sunday mornings, is particularly popular among locals and visitors alike.

Art and Crafts:

Bordeaux has a vibrant artistic scene, and you can find unique pieces of art and crafts to bring home as souvenirs. The Marché des Quais, held every Sunday along the Garonne River, showcases local artists and artisans selling paintings, sculptures, ceramics, handmade jewelry, and much more. For contemporary art lovers, the CAPC (Contemporary Art Museum of Bordeaux) also houses a gift shop with a selection of art books, prints, and design objects.

Local Souvenirs:

To commemorate your visit to Bordeaux, consider picking up some traditional local souvenirs. Postcards, magnets, and keychains featuring iconic Bordeaux landmarks like the Place de la Bourse or the Pont de Pierre are readily available in tourist shops. For a more unique souvenir, opt for a bottle of Bordeaux wine, a personalized wine label, or a wine-related souvenir like a cork coaster or a wine stopper.

Remember that when shopping in Bordeaux, it's always a good idea to explore the smaller side streets and local markets, as they often hide hidden gems and offer a more authentic experience. Additionally, don't forget to inquire about tax-free shopping if you're a non-European Union resident, as you may be eligible for a refund on VAT (Value Added Tax) for certain purchases.

In conclusion, shopping in Bordeaux is a delightful experience, offering a diverse range of local products and souvenirs. From exquisite wines and gastronomic delights to fashion, antiques, art, and crafts, Bordeaux has something for every taste and preference. So, get ready to indulge in the retail therapy and bring home a piece of Bordeaux's charm.

Events and Festivals in Bordeaux

Bordeaux Wine Festival

Bordeaux, the renowned wine region in southwestern France, is not only celebrated for its exceptional wines but also for its vibrant events and festivals that showcase the rich cultural heritage and gastronomy of the region. One of the most prominent and eagerly anticipated events is the Bordeaux Wine Festival, a grand celebration of Bordeaux's world-famous wines. Let's dive into the details of this extraordinary festival.

The Bordeaux Wine Festival is a biennial event that takes place in Bordeaux, primarily along the banks of the Garonne River. It brings together wine enthusiasts, industry professionals, and tourists from around the globe to indulge in the exquisite flavors of Bordeaux wines. The festival is a fusion of wine tastings, gourmet cuisine, music, and a myriad of cultural activities.

The origins of the Bordeaux Wine Festival can be traced back to the 1980s when the city of Bordeaux initiated a wine exhibition called

"Vinexpo." Over time, Vinexpo evolved into a prestigious international wine fair, attracting professionals from the wine industry. In 1998, Bordeaux decided to create a public event alongside Vinexpo to involve the general public in the celebration of wine. This marked the birth of the Bordeaux Wine Festival, which has since become a flagship event for the city.

The festival spans over several days, usually four to five, and takes place in late June or early July, depending on the year. It provides a unique opportunity for visitors to explore the world of Bordeaux wines, discover new vintages, and interact with winemakers and experts. The festival showcases wines from all over the Bordeaux region, including the Médoc, Saint-Émilion, Pomerol, Graves, and Sauternes appellations.

One of the main attractions of the Bordeaux Wine Festival is the "Wine Road" located on the banks of the Garonne River. This long promenade is lined with pavilions representing various wine regions and châteaux. Visitors can meander through the pavilions, taste a wide range of Bordeaux wines, and engage in conversations with winemakers who are passionate about sharing their expertise. It's a fantastic opportunity to learn about different grape varieties, terroirs, and winemaking techniques directly from the source.

Apart from the wine tastings, the festival offers a myriad of cultural and culinary experiences. Visitors can indulge in gourmet food prepared by renowned local chefs, with dishes specifically crafted to complement Bordeaux wines. Food stalls and pop-up restaurants showcase the region's gastronomic delights, such as oysters from Arcachon Bay, traditional cheeses, and delectable pastries.

The Bordeaux Wine Festival also hosts numerous cultural events, including live music performances, art exhibitions, and theatrical shows. The festival's ambiance is lively and convivial, with a festive atmosphere permeating the entire city. Visitors can enjoy concerts by renowned artists, participate in workshops on wine and food pairing, and witness spectacular firework displays that illuminate the Garonne River.

To enhance the experience further, the Bordeaux Wine Festival incorporates various activities that highlight the natural beauty and historical heritage of the city. River cruises allow visitors to admire Bordeaux's iconic architecture, including the stunning 18th-century buildings of the Place de la Bourse. Guided tours take wine enthusiasts to nearby vineyards, offering an immersive experience in the wine-growing process and the opportunity to witness the breathtaking landscapes that shape Bordeaux's wine production.

In summary, the Bordeaux Wine Festival is a captivating celebration that allows visitors to dive deep into the world of Bordeaux wines, savor exceptional flavors, and immerse themselves in the cultural tapestry of the region. Whether you are a wine connoisseur, a food lover, or simply someone looking to experience the joie de vivre of Bordeaux, this festival promises an unforgettable journey through the rich traditions and flavors that make Bordeaux wines truly extraordinary.

Bordeaux Fête le Fleuve

Bordeaux, located in the southwest of France, is a vibrant city known for its rich history, stunning architecture, and world-renowned wine. Among the many events and festivals that take place in Bordeaux throughout the year, one of the most notable and highly anticipated is Bordeaux Fête le Fleuve.

Bordeaux Fête le Fleuve, which translates to "Bordeaux Celebrates the River," is an annual festival that celebrates the city's close relationship with the Garonne River, which flows through the heart of Bordeaux. The festival aims to promote the cultural, artistic, and environmental significance of the river, while also providing a platform for entertainment, recreation, and education.

The festival typically takes place over several days in the summer, attracting both locals and tourists from around the world. It features a diverse range of activities and events that cater to people of all ages and interests. Here are some key highlights of Bordeaux Fête le Fleuve:

Nautical Parades: The festival kicks off with magnificent nautical parades on the Garonne River, showcasing an array of boats, yachts, and historic vessels. This colorful spectacle is a visual feast for spectators, with participants dressed in traditional maritime attire and the river adorned with decorative flags and banners.

Water Activities: Bordeaux Fête le Fleuve offers numerous opportunities to engage in water-based activities, allowing visitors to fully appreciate the beauty and vitality of the river. From boat rides and cruises to kayaking and paddleboarding, there are options for both leisurely exploration and adrenaline-fueled adventures.

Wine Tastings: Given Bordeaux's esteemed reputation as a wine capital, it comes as no surprise that wine plays a prominent role in the festival. Various wine tastings and workshops are organized, providing attendees with the chance to savor the region's finest vintages, learn about winemaking techniques, and discover new flavors.

Culinary Delights: Food lovers are in for a treat at Bordeaux Fête le Fleuve, as the festival showcases the diverse gastronomy of the region. Local chefs and restaurants set up stalls and food trucks, serving up an enticing selection of dishes that highlight the freshest ingredients from land and sea. From gourmet seafood platters to delectable pastries, there's something to satisfy every palate.

Concerts and Performances: The festival stages numerous concerts and performances featuring both local and international artists. From jazz and classical music to contemporary and world music, the lineup is diverse and caters to a wide range of musical tastes. These performances take place in various venues, including outdoor stages along the riverbanks, creating a lively and electric atmosphere.

Fireworks and Light Shows: As the sun sets, Bordeaux Fête le Fleuve illuminates the city's skyline with breathtaking fireworks and light shows. The vibrant colors and dazzling effects create a magical ambiance, captivating spectators and providing a grand finale to each day of the festival.

Environmental Awareness: Bordeaux Fête le Fleuve also focuses on raising awareness about environmental issues and promoting sustainable practices. Workshops, conferences, and exhibitions are held to educate visitors about the importance of preserving the river's ecosystem and encouraging responsible tourism.

Throughout Bordeaux Fête le Fleuve, the entire city comes alive with a festive spirit. Streets are adorned with decorations, local businesses offer special promotions, and cultural events spill into the surrounding neighborhoods. The festival serves as a testament to Bordeaux's passion for its heritage, its vibrant cultural scene, and its commitment to environmental stewardship.

In conclusion, Bordeaux Fête le Fleuve is an annual celebration that showcases the beauty of the Garonne River and the cultural richness of Bordeaux. With its wide range of activities, including nautical parades, water sports, wine tastings, concerts, and light shows, the festival provides an immersive and unforgettable experience for visitors. Whether you're a history enthusiast, a food lover, a music aficionado, or simply someone seeking a joyful atmosphere, Bordeaux Fête le Fleuve is a must-visit event that perfectly captures the essence of this remarkable city.

Bordeaux International Fireworks Competition

The Bordeaux International Fireworks Competition is an extraordinary annual event that takes place in the beautiful city of Bordeaux, France. Known for its rich heritage, exquisite wines, and stunning architecture, Bordeaux adds another feather to its cap with this dazzling display of fireworks. The competition attracts participants from all over the world, creating a mesmerizing spectacle that delights locals and visitors alike. This article provides a comprehensive overview of the Bordeaux International Fireworks Competition, including its history, location, schedule, and the experience it offers to attendees.

History:

The Bordeaux International Fireworks Competition has a long-standing tradition that dates back to its inception in 1996. Initially conceived as a local event, it gradually gained international recognition and evolved into a prestigious competition that showcases the best pyrotechnic talents from across the globe. Over the years, the competition has become an integral part of Bordeaux's cultural calendar, attracting thousands of spectators each year.

Location:
The competition takes place against the stunning backdrop of the Garonne River, right in the heart of Bordeaux. The riverside location provides a unique setting for the fireworks, with the lights reflecting off the water and illuminating the city's landmarks. Spectators can enjoy the show from various vantage points along the riverbanks, such as the Quai Louis XVIII or the Place de la Bourse, where the renowned Miroir d'Eau (Water Mirror) adds an extra touch of magic to the display.

Schedule and Format:
The Bordeaux International Fireworks Competition typically takes place during the summer months, spanning several weekends from June to August. Each weekend features a different participating country, with expert pyrotechnic teams competing against each other to create the most impressive and visually captivating fireworks display. The competition usually culminates with a grand finale where the winners are announced.

Experience for Attendees:
Attending the Bordeaux International Fireworks Competition is a truly memorable

experience. The vibrant atmosphere, the anticipation of each display, and the joyous crowd all contribute to an unforgettable evening. The fireworks themselves are meticulously choreographed to music, creating a synchronized symphony of light and sound that leaves spectators in awe. The pyrotechnic teams skillfully blend a range of effects, from dazzling bursts of color to intricate patterns and shapes, ensuring a breathtaking spectacle that appeals to people of all ages.

Tips for Visitors:

Arrive Early: Given the popularity of the event, it is advisable to arrive early to secure a good viewing spot along the riverbanks. Consider bringing picnic blankets or folding chairs to ensure comfort during the show.

Check the Schedule: Stay updated on the competition's schedule and participating countries to plan your visit accordingly. Each display offers a unique artistic interpretation, so attending multiple weekends can provide a diverse experience.

Explore Bordeaux: While attending the fireworks competition, take advantage of your visit to explore the city of Bordeaux. Discover its architectural gems, sample its world-renowned wines, and immerse yourself in its vibrant cultural scene.

Conclusion:

The Bordeaux International Fireworks Competition is a magnificent celebration that showcases the artistry and creativity of pyrotechnic experts from around the world. Against the backdrop of Bordeaux's picturesque riverside, attendees are treated to an unforgettable display of lights, colors, and sounds. Whether you are a local resident or a visitor, this event offers a magical experience that will leave you in awe of the beauty and spectacle of fireworks. Make sure to mark your calendars and join the thousands of spectators who gather annually to witness this extraordinary event in Bordeaux.

Bordeaux Marathon

The Bordeaux Marathon is an eagerly anticipated annual event that takes place in the charming city of Bordeaux, France. Known for its rich history, stunning architecture, and world-renowned vineyards, Bordeaux serves as the perfect backdrop for this thrilling race. The marathon attracts thousands of participants from around the globe, ranging from professional athletes to amateur runners, all eager to challenge themselves and experience the beauty of Bordeaux.

Event Overview:
The Bordeaux Marathon is a classic 42.195-kilometer race that traverses through the scenic streets of Bordeaux, showcasing the city's remarkable landmarks and picturesque landscapes. The event is organized with great care and precision, ensuring a seamless and enjoyable experience for both runners and spectators. The marathon is typically held on a Sunday in the spring, taking advantage of Bordeaux's pleasant climate and lush surroundings.

Race Course:
The race course of the Bordeaux Marathon is thoughtfully designed to provide a unique and unforgettable experience for the participants. It takes runners on a journey through the heart of Bordeaux, encompassing both historic and contemporary elements of the city. The course starts and finishes in a central location, often near one of Bordeaux's iconic landmarks, such

as Place de la Bourse or the stunning Bordeaux Cathedral.

As runners progress along the course, they are treated to breathtaking views of Bordeaux's architectural wonders, including the Place des Quinconces, Pont de Pierre, and the magnificent Garonne River. The route also winds through the charming narrow streets of the historic district, allowing participants to soak in the city's rich heritage and vibrant atmosphere.

Festival Atmosphere:
The Bordeaux Marathon is not just a race; it is a celebration of sport, community, and the unique spirit of Bordeaux. The entire city comes alive during the marathon weekend, creating a festive atmosphere that embraces both participants and spectators. Local residents line the streets, cheering on the runners and offering words of encouragement, contributing to the electrifying ambiance.

Moreover, the event often features live music performances, entertainment, and food stalls, adding to the overall festive vibe. Participants and their families can enjoy a range of activities and attractions throughout the weekend, creating a memorable experience beyond the race itself.

Participant Experience:
The Bordeaux Marathon caters to runners of all levels, from seasoned athletes seeking personal bests to first-time marathoners eager to conquer a new challenge. The event offers a variety of registration options, including individual entries, team relays, and shorter distances like the half-marathon and 10K races. This inclusiveness makes the marathon accessible to a wide range of participants, fostering a sense of camaraderie among the running community.

To ensure the safety and comfort of all participants, the event organizers provide well-stocked aid stations along the course, offering hydration and nutrition. Medical personnel and volunteers are also strategically positioned to provide assistance if needed. The race is professionally timed, allowing runners to track their progress and compare their performance with fellow participants.

Post-Race Celebrations:
Upon crossing the finish line, participants are greeted with an overwhelming sense of

accomplishment and the warm embrace of an enthusiastic crowd. Finishers receive well-deserved medals, commemorating their achievement in completing the Bordeaux Marathon. Post-race celebrations include a lively awards ceremony, where top performers in various categories are honored and celebrated.

Beyond the race, runners can explore the vibrant city of Bordeaux, savoring its world-class cuisine, sampling exquisite wines, and indulging in the rich cultural offerings. The marathon weekend often coincides with other local events, allowing participants to fully immerse themselves in the vibrant atmosphere of Bordeaux.

Conclusion:
The Bordeaux Marathon is an exceptional event that combines athleticism, scenic beauty, and the spirit of Bordeaux. Whether you are a dedicated runner or a passionate spectator, this race offers an incredible opportunity to explore the city's cultural treasures while participating in a challenging and rewarding sporting event. The Bordeaux Marathon truly embodies the essence of Bordeaux's charm, creating memories that will last a lifetime.

Other Cultural and Music Festivals

Bordeaux, the vibrant city in southwestern France, is not only known for its world-class wines and beautiful architecture but also for its rich cultural scene. Throughout the year, Bordeaux hosts a variety of events and festivals, including a range of cultural and music festivals that cater to diverse tastes and interests. From classical music and jazz to contemporary art and dance, there is something for everyone to enjoy. Here are some of the notable cultural and music festivals in Bordeaux:

Bordeaux Wine Festival: As a city renowned for its wine production, it comes as no surprise that Bordeaux hosts an exceptional wine festival. Held every two years in odd-numbered years, the Bordeaux Wine Festival celebrates the region's vineyards and winemaking traditions. Visitors can enjoy tastings of Bordeaux's finest wines, attend workshops, and participate in various wine-related activities. The festival takes place along the banks of the Garonne River, offering a stunning backdrop for the festivities.

Bordeaux Métropole Festival: This annual festival is a true celebration of arts and culture, encompassing a wide range of disciplines including music, theater, dance, visual arts, and more. The Bordeaux Métropole Festival takes place over several weeks and features performances by national and international artists at various venues throughout the city. From classical concerts in historic churches to contemporary art exhibitions in cultural centers, this festival showcases the city's vibrant artistic scene.

Bordeaux International Organ Festival: Held each summer, the Bordeaux International Organ Festival is a must-visit event for classical music enthusiasts. The festival brings together renowned organists from around the world who showcase their skills on the magnificent organs found in Bordeaux's historic churches. Concerts are held in venues such as the Saint-André Cathedral and the Basilica of Saint-Michel, providing a unique opportunity to experience the power and beauty of organ music in a truly majestic setting.

Bordeaux Jazz Festival: Jazz lovers will find their groove at the Bordeaux Jazz Festival, an annual event that attracts both established artists and emerging talents from the jazz world. Spread across several venues in the city, the festival offers a diverse program featuring a range of jazz styles, from traditional to avant-garde. Attendees can enjoy performances by acclaimed musicians, participate in jam sessions, and experience the vibrant atmosphere of Bordeaux's jazz scene.

Novart Bordeaux: Novart Bordeaux is a multidisciplinary festival that celebrates contemporary art in all its forms. Taking place over several weeks, the festival showcases innovative works by visual artists, performers, dancers, and musicians. The events are held in various venues, including galleries, museums, and public spaces, and aim to engage audiences through thought-provoking and immersive experiences. Novart Bordeaux pushes the boundaries of artistic expression, making it a must-see festival for those seeking cutting-edge contemporary art.

Bordeaux Rock Festival: For music enthusiasts who prefer alternative and indie sounds, the Bordeaux Rock Festival offers a platform for emerging artists in the rock, pop, and electronic genres. The festival features a mix of local talent and national/international acts, providing an exciting lineup of performances. From intimate club shows to larger outdoor stages, the Bordeaux Rock Festival offers a dynamic and energetic atmosphere where attendees can discover new music and enjoy live performances.

These are just a few examples of the cultural and music festivals that take place in Bordeaux. The city's vibrant arts scene ensures that there are numerous events throughout the year, catering to various tastes and interests. Whether you are a wine enthusiast, a lover of classical music, a jazz aficionado, or an art enthusiast, Bordeaux's festivals provide an enriching cultural experience that showcases the city's creativity and artistic spirit.

Practical Information

Emergency Contacts

When traveling to Bordeaux, France, it is important to familiarize yourself with the emergency contact information. Although Bordeaux is a relatively safe city, emergencies can happen, and being prepared with the right contacts can help ensure your safety and well-being. Here is a detailed guide to the emergency contacts you should be aware of in Bordeaux:

General Emergency Number:
In case of any life-threatening situation or when you require immediate assistance from the police, fire department, or medical services, dial 112. This number is the general emergency number in France and can be accessed from any mobile or landline phone. When you call 112, a dispatcher will assess your situation and dispatch the appropriate emergency services.

Medical Emergencies:
a. SAMU (Service d'Aide Médicale Urgente) - Dial 15: If you or someone around you requires urgent medical attention or an ambulance, dial 15. SAMU is the French emergency medical

service, and they provide rapid response and medical advice over the phone.

b. SOS Médecins Bordeaux - +33 (0)5 56 44 74 74: SOS Médecins is a network of doctors who provide medical assistance at home, including during weekends and public holidays. They can be contacted when you require medical attention but it is not an immediate emergency.

Police and Law Enforcement:
a. Police Nationale - Dial 17: If you need to report a crime, require police assistance, or need to file a complaint, dial 17 to reach the French National Police.

b. Gendarmerie Nationale - +33 (0)5 57 85 71 20: The Gendarmerie is a branch of the French armed forces responsible for public safety. They handle a wide range of law enforcement issues, including traffic control and certain criminal investigations.

Fire Department:
To report a fire or any other emergency related to fire, dial 18. The fire department, known as Sapeurs-Pompiers, is responsible for firefighting, rescue operations, and emergency medical assistance in case of accidents.

European Emergency Number:

In addition to the local emergency numbers, it is worth noting that the European emergency number, 112, can also be dialed from any mobile or landline phone. This number will connect you to emergency services in any EU member state, including France.

Remember, it is always a good idea to have a basic understanding of the local language or have access to translation services when contacting emergency services in Bordeaux. Furthermore, keep your personal identification and travel documents in a safe place, and have a copy of them readily available in case of emergencies.

It is also recommended to check with your embassy or consulate for any specific emergency assistance services they might provide to citizens traveling in Bordeaux.

By being aware of these emergency contacts and having them readily available, you can ensure that you are prepared to handle any unforeseen circumstances and receive the necessary help while visiting Bordeaux, France.

Useful Phrases

When traveling to Bordeaux, France, it's always helpful to have a few key phrases in the local language to enhance your experience and make communication easier. While many people in Bordeaux can speak English, making an effort to speak some basic French phrases will be appreciated by locals and can help you navigate various situations more smoothly. Here are some useful phrases to keep in mind:

Greetings and Basic Expressions:
- Bonjour (bohn-zhoor) - Hello / Good day
- Bonsoir (bohn-swahr) - Good evening
- Merci (mehr-see) - Thank you
- S'il vous plaît (see-voo-pleh) - Please
- Excusez-moi (ehk-skew-zay-mwah) - Excuse me
- Au revoir (oh ruh-vwahr) - Goodbye

Getting Around:
- Où est...? (oo ay) - Where is...?
- La gare (lah gar) - The train station
- L'aéroport (lah-ay-roh-por) - The airport
- Le centre-ville (luh sahn-truh-veel) - The city center

- Un taxi, s'il vous plaît (uhn tah-ksee, see-voo-pleh) - A taxi, please
- Je cherche... (zhuh shehrsh) - I'm looking for...

Food and Drink:
- Une table pour deux, s'il vous plaît (oohn tahbl poor duh, see-voo-pleh) - A table for two, please
- Le menu, s'il vous plaît (luh muh-noo, see-voo-pleh) - The menu, please
- Je voudrais... (zhuh voo-dreh) - I would like...
- L'addition, s'il vous plaît (lah-dee-syon, see-voo-pleh) - The bill, please
- Une bouteille de vin (oohn boo-tayl duh van) - A bottle of wine

Shopping:
- Combien ça coûte? (kohm-byahn sah koot) - How much does it cost?
- Je voudrais essayer celui-ci (zhuh voo-dreh ess-ay-yay suh-lee-see) - I would like to try this one
- Je suis intéressé(e) par... (zhuh swee zahn-tay-ray pahr) - I am interested in...
- Est-ce que vous avez...? (ess-kuh voo zah-veh) - Do you have...?

Emergency Situations:
Au secours! (oh suh-koor) - Help!
Je ne me sens pas bien (zhuh nuh muh sah pah byahn) - I don't feel well
Appelez la police (ah-puh-lay lah poh-lees) - Call the police
Où est l'hôpital le plus proche? (oo ay loh-pee-tahl luh ploo prosh) - Where is the nearest hospital?

Remember, when using these phrases, it's important to speak politely and with a smile. French culture values politeness and courtesy, so a friendly attitude will go a long way in your interactions.

Additionally, it's worth noting that different regions in France may have variations in pronunciation or local expressions, but these phrases should generally be understood in Bordeaux.

Don't be afraid to give French a try, even if you're not fluent. Locals appreciate the effort and will often be happy to assist you in English if needed. Enjoy your time in Bordeaux, and bonne chance (good luck) with your language endeavors!

Safety Tips

Bordeaux, known for its stunning architecture, world-class wine, and vibrant cultural scene, is a popular destination for tourists from around the world. While Bordeaux is generally a safe city, it's always important to take precautions and be aware of your surroundings. By following some simple safety tips, you can ensure a smooth and enjoyable experience during your visit to Bordeaux. Here are some practical safety tips to keep in mind:

Stay Alert and Be Aware: Like any other city, it's essential to stay alert and aware of your surroundings. Pay attention to the people around you, especially in crowded areas and tourist hotspots. Keep an eye on your belongings at all times, especially in busy places like train stations, markets, and public transportation.

Pickpocketing and Theft: While Bordeaux is not notorious for pickpocketing, it's always wise to take precautions. Keep your valuables secure, preferably in a zipped bag or hidden pockets. Avoid displaying expensive jewelry, cameras, or large amounts of cash, as it may attract unwanted attention. Be cautious in crowded places, particularly in trams, buses, and train stations.

Transportation Safety: Bordeaux has a reliable public transportation system, including trams, buses, and trains. When using public transport, be aware of your surroundings and keep an eye on your belongings. Avoid using unlicensed taxis and make sure to book reliable services. If you're renting a car, park it in well-lit and secure areas, and avoid leaving valuables inside.

Nighttime Safety: Bordeaux has a vibrant nightlife, especially in areas like Place de la Victoire and Quai de Paludate. While enjoying the nightlife, it's important to take precautions. Stick to well-lit and busy areas, and avoid walking alone late at night, especially in unfamiliar neighborhoods. Consider taking a taxi or using rideshare services for added safety.

Emergency Services: Familiarize yourself with the emergency contact numbers in Bordeaux. The general emergency number in France is 112, which can be dialed for police, ambulance, or fire services. Additionally, know the location of the nearest police station and hospital to your accommodation.

Cultural Sensitivity: Bordeaux is a diverse city, and it's important to be respectful of local customs and traditions. Familiarize yourself with the local etiquette and cultural norms to avoid any unintentional offenses. Dress appropriately, especially when visiting religious sites, and be mindful of local sensitivities.

Health and Medical Facilities: Bordeaux has excellent healthcare facilities, including hospitals and clinics. It's advisable to have comprehensive travel insurance that covers medical expenses. Carry any necessary prescription medications with you, along with a copy of your prescriptions, in case you need refills or medical assistance.

Natural Hazards: Bordeaux is not prone to major natural disasters, but it's always wise to stay informed about potential weather conditions. In case of severe weather, follow local authorities' instructions and stay updated through reliable sources, such as local news channels or official websites.

Use Reliable Information Sources: When seeking information about attractions, events, or transportation, rely on official sources or reputable websites. Tourist information centers are also available throughout the city and can provide accurate and up-to-date information.

Remember, these safety tips are meant to enhance your overall experience and ensure a trouble-free stay in Bordeaux. By staying vigilant, being aware of your surroundings, and taking necessary precautions, you can fully enjoy all that Bordeaux has to offer while prioritizing your safety and well-being.

Transportation Information

Bordeaux, located in southwestern France, is a vibrant and picturesque city known for its wine, stunning architecture, and rich cultural heritage. When it comes to transportation, Bordeaux offers a range of options to help visitors and residents explore the city and its surrounding areas. Here is some practical information on transportation in Bordeaux:

Bordeaux-Mérignac Airport:

Bordeaux-Mérignac Airport (BOD) is the main international airport serving Bordeaux. It is located approximately 12 kilometers west of the city center. The airport offers domestic and international flights, connecting Bordeaux to various destinations across Europe and beyond. From the airport, you can reach the city center by various means of transportation, including taxis, shuttle buses, and public transportation.

Public Transportation:
The public transportation network in Bordeaux is extensive and efficient, making it easy to navigate the city and its suburbs. The primary modes of public transportation include trams, buses, and a bike-sharing system.

Trams: Bordeaux has an extensive tram network consisting of four lines (A, B, C, and D). Trams are a convenient and reliable way to get around the city. They operate from early morning until midnight, with extended hours on weekends and public holidays.

Buses: The bus network in Bordeaux complements the tram system and provides connectivity to areas not served by trams. Buses operate from early morning until midnight, with reduced service on Sundays and public holidays.

V^3 Bike-Sharing: Bordeaux offers a popular bike-sharing system called V^3. With numerous bike stations scattered across the city, you can easily rent a bike for short trips. The system operates 24/7, and you can purchase a short-term or long-term subscription.

Taxis and Ride-Sharing Services:
Taxis are readily available throughout Bordeaux, and they provide a convenient mode of transportation, especially for late-night travel or when carrying heavy luggage. You can find taxi stands at popular locations or hail a cab on the street. Additionally, ride-sharing services like Uber are also available in Bordeaux.

Car Rental:
If you prefer to have more flexibility and independence in your travels, renting a car in Bordeaux is an option worth considering. Several car rental companies operate in the city, and you can choose from a range of vehicles to suit your needs. It's important to note that parking in the city center can be limited and expensive, so it's advisable to

familiarize yourself with parking regulations and consider using public transportation for inner-city travel.

Train Travel:
Bordeaux is well-connected to other cities in France and Europe by train. The city's main train station is Gare de Bordeaux-Saint-Jean, located in the city center. High-speed trains, such as the TGV, provide fast and convenient connections to destinations like Paris, Lyon, Marseille, and beyond.

Ferries and River Cruises:
Bordeaux is situated on the Garonne River, and several companies offer river cruises and ferry services along the waterway. These cruises provide a unique perspective of the city and its surroundings, allowing you to enjoy the scenic beauty of the region.

Walking and Cycling:
Bordeaux is a pedestrian-friendly city with many attractions within walking distance of each other. Exploring the city center on foot is a pleasant experience, allowing you to appreciate its charming streets, squares, and architecture. Additionally, Bordeaux has

dedicated cycling lanes, making it an excellent city for cycling enthusiasts.

In conclusion, Bordeaux provides a comprehensive transportation network, including airports, trams, buses, taxis, car rentals, trains, and river transportation options. With these various modes of transportation at your disposal, getting around Bordeaux and exploring its treasures is both convenient and enjoyable.

Local Customs and Etiquette

When visiting Bordeaux, it's essential to familiarize yourself with the local customs and etiquette to ensure a pleasant and respectful experience. Here is a detailed guide to local customs and etiquette in Bordeaux, France:

Greetings and Politeness:

- When meeting someone for the first time, it is customary to greet them with a handshake, accompanied by a polite "Bonjour" (Good day) or "Bonsoir"

(Good evening), depending on the time of day.
- French people appreciate the use of "s'il vous plaît" (please) and "merci" (thank you) in everyday interactions, so make sure to use these phrases frequently.
- When entering a shop or establishment, it is considered polite to greet the staff with a simple "Bonjour" to acknowledge their presence.

Punctuality:

- Being punctual is highly valued in French culture. If you have an appointment or are meeting someone, it is best to arrive on time or even a few minutes early to show respect for their time.

Dining Etiquette:

- When dining at a restaurant, it is customary to wait to be seated by the host or hostess.
- Keep in mind that the French typically have a leisurely dining experience and appreciate taking their time during meals. Avoid rushing through your meal

or requesting the bill immediately after finishing.

- When ordering, address the waiter or waitress with a polite "s'il vous plaît" before making your request.
- The French take their food seriously, so avoid asking for any modifications to the dish, unless you have dietary restrictions or allergies.
- It is customary to keep your hands on the table during the meal, but avoid resting your elbows on the table.
- When finished with your meal, place your utensils together on the plate, with the handles facing right, to indicate that you have finished eating.

Wine Tasting:

- Bordeaux is renowned for its exceptional wines, so if you have the opportunity to visit vineyards or participate in wine tastings, there are a few etiquettes to keep in mind.
- Hold the wine glass by the stem rather than the bowl to prevent the wine from warming up.
- When tasting multiple wines, it is customary to take small sips and swirl

the wine in the glass to aerate it before evaluating its aroma and taste.
- Remember to spit out the wine after tasting, especially if you are sampling several wines in one session, to avoid intoxication.

Dress Code:

French people tend to dress elegantly and stylishly, even in casual settings. It is advisable to dress neatly and avoid overly casual attire when visiting Bordeaux.
When visiting religious sites or monuments, it is respectful to dress modestly, covering your shoulders and knees.

Public Etiquette:

- In public spaces such as streets, parks, or public transportation, it is important to be mindful of your noise level and avoid causing disturbances.
- When using public transportation, offer your seat to the elderly, pregnant women, or individuals with disabilities.

Language:

- While English is spoken to some extent in tourist areas, attempting to speak a few basic French phrases will be appreciated by the locals. Simple greetings and phrases like "Excusez-moi" (Excuse me) and "Parlez-vous anglais?" (Do you speak English?) can go a long way.
- By following these local customs and etiquette guidelines, you'll demonstrate respect for Bordeaux's culture and people while enjoying a memorable visit to this beautiful city in France.

Conclusion

As our travelers reach the concluding chapter of "Bordeaux France Travel Guide," they find themselves immersed in the final moments of their captivating journey through the renowned region of Bordeaux. The air is filled with the intoxicating aroma of history, art, and wine, as they delve deeper into the secrets that lie within this picturesque destination.

Their exploration begins in the heart of Bordeaux's historic city center, where the travelers are immediately captivated by the beauty of the cobblestone streets, ornate buildings, and charming squares. The guide introduces them to the city's rich heritage, tracing its origins back to Roman times. They wander through narrow alleys, discovering hidden gems like the Gothic Cathédrale Saint-André and the opulent Grand Théâtre, which stand as testaments to Bordeaux's architectural grandeur.

Continuing their journey, the travelers are led into the vibrant cultural scene of Bordeaux. The guide unravels tales of artistic heritage as they explore renowned art museums, such as the Musée des Beaux-Arts, where masterpieces by Delacroix, Rubens, and Monet adorn the walls. The contemporary art installations at the CAPC musée d'art contemporain showcase Bordeaux's commitment to innovation and creativity, leaving the visitors inspired by the city's artistic prowess.

No exploration of Bordeaux would be complete without venturing into its world-famous vineyards. The travelers embark on a fascinating odyssey through rolling hills and picturesque landscapes, immersing themselves in the art of winemaking. The guide enlightens them about the complex wine classification system and the distinct characteristics of each appellation. With every sip, the travelers learn to distinguish the subtle nuances of Bordeaux's reds, whites, and sweet wines, gaining a deeper appreciation for the craftsmanship that has made Bordeaux a revered wine region for centuries.

Bordeaux's culinary scene is a delightful part of the journey. The guide invites the travelers to indulge in a gastronomic adventure, exploring Michelin-starred restaurants and quaint local eateries. They savor traditional Bordeaux delicacies such as entrecôte bordelaise, cannelés, and a variety of cheeses. The fusion of old and new flavors captivates their taste buds as modern chefs experiment with international influences, adding a contemporary touch to Bordeaux's culinary traditions.

As the story nears its end, the guide unveils Bordeaux's exciting future. The travelers glimpse the innovative urban projects that are reshaping the city's landscape, from the sleek waterfront promenade to the sustainable architecture initiatives. Bordeaux's commitment to environmental conservation and its emergence as a hub for technology and entrepreneurship fill the travelers with anticipation for what lies ahead.

In the epilogue, readers reflect on their journey through the pages of "Bordeaux France Travel Guide." A mix of awe, nostalgia, and a longing for more fills their hearts. The guide has taken them on an unforgettable voyage, unraveling the layers of history, art, and wine that make Bordeaux so captivating. It leaves them inspired to return, armed with newfound knowledge and a deeper appreciation for the region's timeless beauty.

The conclusion of this travel guide is not merely an end but a beginning—a catalyst for travelers to create their own stories within Bordeaux's ancient streets and vineyard-covered hills. It encourages them to embark on their own adventures, ready to explore the essence of Bordeaux and add their own chapters to its rich tapestry of experiences.

Manufactured by Amazon.ca
Acheson, AB